The Wisdom of Maati

Fourth Edition - Expanded

"Those who live today will die tomorrow, those who die tomorrow will be born again; Those who live MAAT will not die."

"The wise person who acts with MAAT is free of falsehood and disorder."

"MAAT is great and it's effectiveness lasting; it has not been disturbed since the time of Asar. There is punishment for those who pass over its laws, but this is unfamiliar to the covetous one....When the end is near, MAAT lasts."

"No one reaches the beneficent West (enlightenment-immortality) unless their heart is righteous by doing MAAT. There is no distinction made between the inferior and the superior person; it only matters that one is found faultless when the balances and the two weights stand before the Lord of Eternity. No one is free from the reckoning. Djehuti, a baboon, holds the balances to count each one according to what they have done upon earth."

"They who revere MAAT are long lived; they who are covetous have no tomb."

Ancient Egyptian Proverbs on
The Philosophy of Maat

P.O.Box 570459
Miami, Florida, 33257
(305) 378-6253 Fax: (305) 378-6253

First U.S. edition 1996
Second edition © 1997 By Reginald Muata Ashby
Third Edition © 2002 By Reginald Muata Ashby
Fourth Edition © 2005 By Reginald Muata Ashby

The author is available for group lectures and individual counseling. For further information contact the publisher.

Ashby, Muata
The Wisdom of Maati ISBN: 1-884564-20-8

Library of Congress Cataloging in Publication Data

1 Yoga 2 Egyptian Philosophy, 3 Eastern Philosophy, 4 Esoterism, 5 Meditation, 6 Self Help.

Cruzian Mystic Books

Also by Muata Ashby

Egyptian Yoga: The Philosophy of Enlightenment
Initiation Into Egyptian Yoga: The Secrets of Sheti
Egyptian Proverbs: Tempt Tchaas,
Mystical Wisdom Teachings and Meditations
The Egyptian Yoga Exercise Workout Book
For more listings see the back section.

SHETAUT NETER©

Based on the book

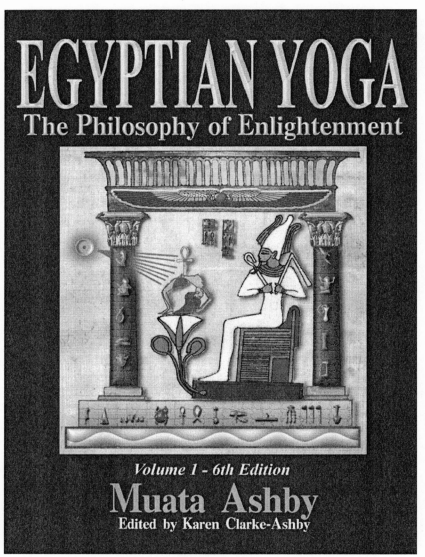

Egyptian Yoga:
The Philosophy of Enlightenment
by
Dr. Reginald Muata Abhaya Ashby

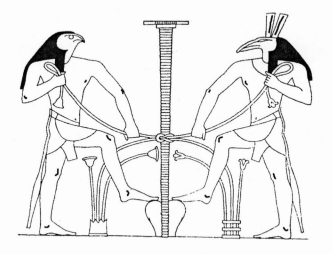

Sema
Institute of Yoga

Sema (⌇) is an Ancient Egyptian word and symbol meaning *union*. The Sema Institute is dedicated to the propagation of the universal teachings of spiritual evolution which relate to the union of humanity and the union of all things within the universe. It is a non-denominational organization which recognizes the unifying principles in all spiritual and religious systems of evolution throughout the world. Our primary goals are to provide the wisdom of ancient spiritual teachings in books, courses and other forms of communication. Secondly, to provide expert instruction and training in the various yogic disciplines including Ancient Egyptian Philosophy, Christian Gnosticism, Indian Philosophy and modern science. Thirdly, to promote world peace and Universal Love.

A primary focus of our tradition is to identify and acknowledge the yogic principles within all religions and to relate them to each other in order to promote their deeper understanding as well as to show the essential unity of purpose and the unity of all living beings and nature within the whole of existence.

The Institute is open to all who believe in the principles of peace, non-violence and spiritual emancipation regardless of sex, race, or creed.

About the author and editor:
Dr. Muata Abhaya Ashby

About The Author

Reginald Muata Ashby holds a Doctor of Philosophy Degree in Religion, and a Doctor of Divinity Degree in Holistic Healing. He is also a Pastoral Counselor and Teacher of Yoga Philosophy and Discipline. Dr. Ashby is an adjunct faculty member of the American Institute of Holistic Theology and an ordained Minister. Dr. Ashby has studied advanced Jnana, Bhakti and Kundalini Yogas under the guidance of Swami Jyotirmayananda, a world renowned Yoga Master. He has studied the mystical teachings of Ancient Egypt for many years and is the creator of the Egyptian Yoga concept. He is also the founder of the Sema Institute, an organization dedicated to the propagation of the teachings of Yoga and mystical spirituality.

Karen Clarke-Ashby, "Vijaya-Asha", is the wife and spiritual partner of Muata. She is an independent researcher, practitioner and teacher of Yoga, a Doctor in the Sciences and a Pastoral Counselor, author of *Yoga Mystic Metaphors,* the editor of Egyptian Proverbs and Egyptian Yoga by Muata. ☥

Sema Institute
P.O. Box 570459, Miami, Fla. 33257 (305) 378-6253, Fax (305) 378-6253
©2002

The Path of Action and Enlightenment

TABLE OF CONTENTS

Author's Foreword

In order to gain a feel for the special subject of this volume it will be necessary to gain a basic knowledge of who the originators of the philosophy of Maat were. The Ancient Egyptians created the vast temples and pyramids as offerings to the Divine and places where the philosophy of Maat was taught. This ancient philosophy was actually part of an even more vast teaching of spirituality called Shetaut Neter. Maat actually is the basis of Shetaut Neter or Ancient Egyptian Religion. Therefore, we will begin with the essential elements of Ancient Egyptian History, Yoga Philosophy and their influence on world mythology and religion. Further on in the text we will present a summary of the Ancient Egyptian Myth of Asar (Osiris), which is the underlying basis of all spiritual practices of Ancient Egypt. Then we will begin a more in depth introduction to Maat Philosophy the reader will thereby have a basis for the study and practice of the science of action. The purpose of this study is to understand how actions lead a human being to experience the consequences in life that are engendered by their own feelings, desires and thoughts. This is the teaching of "Ari" or Karma as it is known to Hindus and Buddhists. We will see how this cosmic law of cause and effect was understood in ancient Africa first by the earliest known civilization, Kamit. (Ancient Egypt) and how we may benefit from this wisdom today and lead ourselves to prosperity, peace and fulfillment.

The purpose of this study

"There are two roads traveled by humankind, those who seek to live MAAT, and those who seek to satisfy their animal passions."

A Brief History of Shetaut Neter

Early Beginnings: The First Religion

Ancient Egypt was the first and most ancient civilization to create a religious system that was complete with all three stages of religion, as well as an advanced spiritual philosophy of righteousness, called Maat Philosophy, that also had secular dimensions. Several temple systems were developed in Kamit; they were all related. The pre-Judaic/Islamic religions that the later Jewish and Muslim religions drew from in order to create their religions developed out of these, ironically enough, only to later repudiate the source from whence they originated. In any case, the Great Sphinx remains the oldest known religious monument in history that denotes high culture and civilization as well. Ancient Egypt and Nubia produced the oldest religious systems and their contact with the rest of the world led to the proliferation of advanced religion and spiritual philosophy. People who were practicing simple animism, shamanism, nature based religions and witchcraft were elevated to the level of not only understanding the nature of the Supreme Being, but also attaining salvation from the miseries of life through the effective discovery of that Transcendental being, not as an untouchable aloof Spirit, but as the very essence of all that exists.

> the Great Sphinx remains the oldest known religious monument in history.

NETERIANISM 10.000 B.C.E. – 2001 A.C.E.

A Long History

For a period spanning over 10,000 years the Neterian religion served the society of ancient Kamit. It is hard to comprehend the vastness of time that is encompassed by Ancient Egyptian culture, religion and philosophy. Yet the evidence is there to be seen by all. It has been collected and presented in the book *African Origins of Civilization, Religion and Yoga Philosophy*. That volume will serve as the historical record for the Neterian religion and as record of its legacy to all humanity. It serves as the basis or foundation for the work contained in all the other books in this series that have been created to elucidate on the teachings and traditions as well as disciplines of the varied Neterian religious traditions.

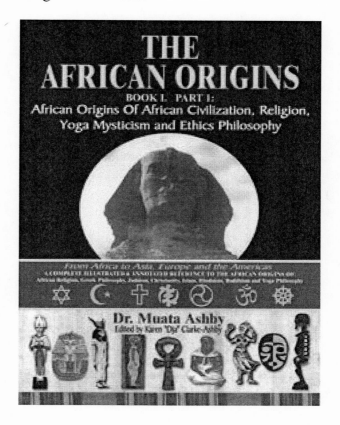

The book *African Origins of Civilization, Religion and Yoga Philosophy,* and the other volumes on the specific traditions detail the philosophies and disciplines that should be practiced by those who want to follow the path of Hm or Hmt, to be practitioners of the Shetaut Neter religion and builders of the Neterian faith worldwide.

Introduction To MAAT PHILOSOPHY

Where Was Shetaut Neter Practiced in Ancient Times?

Below left: A map of North East Africa showing the location of the land of *Ta-Meri* or *Kamit,* also known as Ancient Egypt and South of it is located the land which in modern times is called Sudan.

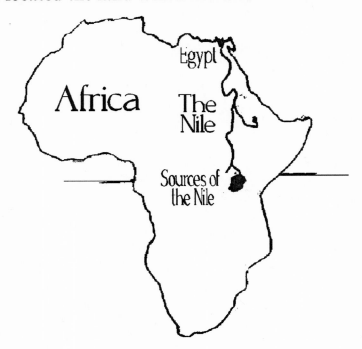

The Land of Kamit in Africa

Above right- The Land of Ancient Egypt-Nile Valley

The cities wherein the major theologies of Neterianism developed were:

A- Sais (temple of Net),
B- Anu (Heliopolis- temple of Ra),
C- Men-nefer or Hetkaptah (Memphis, temple of Ptah),
D- Sakkara (Pyramid Texts),
E- Akhet-Aton (City of Akhenaton, temple of Aton),
F- Abdu (temple of Asar),
G- Denderah (temple of Hetheru),
H- Waset (Thebes, temple of Amun),
I- Edfu (temple of Heru),
J- Philae (temple of Aset). The cities wherein the theology of the Trinity of Asar-Aset-Heru was developed were Anu, Abydos, Philae, Edfu, Denderah and Edfu.

The Path of Action and Enlightenment

The Term Kamit and the Origins of the Ancient Egyptians

Ancient Origins

The Ancient Egyptians recorded that they were originally a colony of Ethiopians from the south who came to the north east part of Africa. The term "Ethiopian," "Nubian," and "Kushite" all relate to the same peoples who lived south of Egypt. In modern times, the land which was once known as Nubia ("Land of Gold"), is currently known as the Sudan, and the land even further south and east towards the coast of east Africa is referred to as Ethiopia (see map above).

Recent research has shown that the modern Nubian word *kiji* means "fertile land, dark gray mud, silt, or black land." Since the sound of this word is close to the Ancient Egyptian name Kish or Kush, referring to the land south of Egypt, it is believed that the name Kush also meant "the land of dark silt" or "the black land." Kush was the Ancient Egyptian name for Nubia. Nubia, the black land, is the Sudan of today. Sudan is an Arabic translation of *sûd* which is the plural form of *aswad*, which means "black," and *ân* which means "of the." So, Sudan means "of the blacks." In the modern Nubian language, *nugud* means "black." Also, *nuger, nugur,* and *nubi* mean "black" as well. All of this indicates that the words Kush, Nubia, and Sudan all mean the same thing — the "black land" and/or the "land of the blacks."[1] As we will see, the differences between the term Kush and the term Kam (Qamit - name for Ancient Egypt in the Ancient Egyptian language) relate more to the same meaning but different geographical locations.

As we have seen, the terms "Ethiopia," "Nubia," "Kush" and "Sudan" all refer to "black land" and/or the "land of the blacks." In the same manner we find that the name of Egypt which was used by the Ancient Egyptians also means "black land" and/or the "land of the blacks." The hieroglyphs below reveal the Ancient Egyptian meaning of the words related to the name of their land. It is clear that the meaning of the word Qamit is equivalent to the word Kush as far as they relate to "black land" and that they also refer to a differentiation in geographical location, i.e. Kush is the "black land of the south" and Qamit is the "black land of the north." Both terms denote the primary quality that defines Africa, "black" or "Blackness" (referring to the land and its people). The quality of blackness and the consonantal sound of K or Q as well as the reference to the land are all aspects of commonality between the Ancient Kushitic and Kamitan terms.

Kush is the "black land of the south" and Qamit is the "black land of the north."

---

[1] "Nubia," *Microsoft® Encarta® Africana.* © 1999 Microsoft Corporation. All rights reserved.

Introduction To MAAT PHILOSOPHY

The Hieroglyphic Text for the Name Qamit

Qamit - Ancient Egypt

Qamit - blackness – black

Qamit - literature of Ancient Egypt – scriptures

Qamiu or variant  -

Ancient Egyptians-people of the black land.

The Path of Action and Enlightenment

When Was Neterian Religion Practiced?

c. 65,000 B.C.E. Paleolithic – Nekhen (Hierakonpolis)
c. 10,000 B.C.E. Neolithic – period

PREDYNASTIC PERIOD

c. 10,500 B.C.E.-7,000 B.C.E. <u>Creation of the Great Sphinx</u> Modern archeological accepted dates – Sphinx means Hor-m-akhet or Heru (Horus) in the horizon. This means that the King is one with the Spirit, Ra as an enlightened person possessing an animal aspect (lion) and illuminated intellect. <u>Anunian Theology – Ra - Serpent Power Spirituality</u>

c. 10,000 B.C.E.-5,500 B.C.E. <u>The Sky GOD- Realm of Light-Day – NETER</u> Androgynous – All-encompassing –Absolute, Nameless Being, later identified with Ra-Herakhti (Sphinx)

>7,000 B.C.E. Kemetic Myth and Theology present in architecture

OLD KINGDOM PERIOD

5500+ B.C.E. to 600 A.C.E. <u>Amun -Ra - Ptah (Horus) – Amenit - Rai – Sekhmet</u> (male and female Trinity-Complementary Opposites)

5500+ B.C.E. <u>Memphite Theology – Ptah</u>

5500+ B.C.E. <u>Hermopolitan Theology- Djehuti</u>

5500+ B.C.E. <u>The Asarian Resurrection Theology - Asar</u>

5500+B.C.E. <u>The Goddess Principle- Theology</u>, Isis-Hathor-Net-Mut-Sekhmet-Buto

5500 B.C.E. (Dynasty 1) Beginning of the Dynastic Period (Unification of Upper and Lower Egypt)

5000 B.C.E. (5th Dynasty) <u>Pyramid Texts - Egyptian Book of Coming Forth By Day - 42 Precepts of MAAT and codification of the Pre-Dynastic theologies</u> (Pre-Dynastic period: 10,000 B.C.E.-5,500 B.C.E.) Coming Forth By Day (Book of the Dead)

5000-4000 B.C.E. WISDOM TEXTS-Precepts of Ptahotep

4241 B.C.E. The Pharaonic (royal) calendar based on the Sothic system (star Sirius) was in use.

Introduction To MAAT PHILOSOPHY

MIDDLE KINGDOM PERIOD

2040 B.C.E.-1786 B.C.E. *COFFIN TEXTS* Coming Forth By Day (Book of the Dead)
1800 B.C.E.-Theban Theology - Amun

NEW KINGDOM PERIOD

1570 B.C.E.-Books of Coming Forth By Day (Book of the Dead)
1353 B.C.E. Atonism- Non-dualist Pre-Dynastic Philosophy was redefined by
 Akhenaton.
712-657 B.C.E. The Nubian Dynasty
657 B.C.E. - 450 A.C.E. This is the last period of Ancient Egyptian culture which
 saw several invasions by foreigners from Asia Minor (Assyrians, Persians)
 and Europe (Greeks and Romans) and finally the closing of the temples,
 murdering of priests and priestesses, the forced conversion to the foreign
 religions and destruction of Neterian holy sites by Christians and Muslims.
 The teaching went dormant at this time until the 20th century A.C.E.

What is Shetaut Neter

The Spiritual Culture and the Purpose of Life: Shetaut Neter

"Men and women are to become God-like through a life of virtue and the cultivation of the spirit through scientific knowledge, practice and bodily discipline."

-Ancient Egyptian Proverb

The highest forms of Joy, Peace and Contentment are obtained when the meaning of life is discovered. When the human being is in harmony then it is possible to reflect and meditate upon the human condition and realize the limitations of worldly pursuits. When there is peace and harmony a human being can practice any of the varied disciplines, designated as Shetaut Neter, to promote the evolution of the human being towards the ultimate goal of life which Spiritual Enlightenment. Spiritual Enlightenment is the awakening of the human being to the awareness of the transcendental essence which binds the universe and which is eternal and immutable. In this discovery is also the sobering and ecstatic realization that the human being is one with that transcendental essence. With this realization come great joy, peace and power to experience the fullness of live and to realize the purpose of life during the time on earth. The lotus is a primary symbol of Shetaut Neter, meaning the turning towards the light of truth, peace and transcendental harmony.

The lotus is a primary symbol of Shetaut Neter

Introduction To MAAT PHILOSOPHY

The Essence of Shetaut Neter

The Ancient Egyptians were African peoples who lived in the north-eastern quadrant of the continent of Africa. They were descendants of the Nubians, who had themselves originated from farther south into the heart of Africa at the great lakes region, the sources of the Nile River. They created a vast civilization and culture earlier than any other society in known history and organized a nation which was based on the concepts of balance and order as well as spiritual enlightenment. These ancient African people called their land Kamit and soon after developing a well ordered society they began to realize that the world is full of wonders but life is fleeting and that there must be something more to human existence. They developed spiritual systems that were designed to allow human beings to understand the nature of this secret being who is the essence of all Creation. They called this spiritual system "Shtaut Ntr."

Shetaut means secret.

Neter means Divinity.

What is Neterianism and Who are the Neterians?

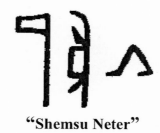

"Shemsu Neter"

"Follower (of) Neter"

The term "Neterianism" is derived from the name "Shetaut Neter." Those who follow the spiritual path of Shetaut Neter are therefore referred to as "Neterians."

The term
"Neterianism"

Neterianism is the science of Neter, that is, the study of the secret or mystery of Neter, the enigma of that which transcends ordinary consciousness but from which all creation arises. The world did not come from nothing, nor is it sustained by nothing. Rather it is a manifestation of that which is beyond time and space but which at the same time permeates and maintains the fundamental elements. In other words, it is the substratum of Creation and the essential nature of all that exists.

So those who follow the Neter may be referred to as Neterians.

Who is Neter?

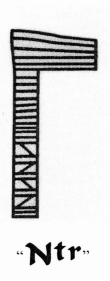

"Ntr"

The symbol of Neter was described by an Ancient Kamitan sage as:

"That which is placed in the coffin"

The term Ntr , or Ntjr , come from the Ancient Egyptian hieroglyphic language which did not record its vowels. However, the term survives in the Coptic language as *"Nutar."* The same Coptic meaning (divine force or sustaining power) applies in the present as it did in ancient times, It is a symbol composed of a wooden staff that was wrapped with strips of fabric, like a mummy. The strips alternate in color with yellow, green and blue. The mummy in Kamitan spirituality is understood to be the dead but resurrected Divinity. So the Nutar is actually every human being who does not really die, but goes to live on in a different form. Further, the resurrected spirit of every human being is that same Divinity. Phonetically, the term Nutar is related to other terms having the same meaning, the latin "Natura," Spanish Naturalesa, English "Nature" and "Nutriment", etc. In a real sense, as we will see, Natur means power manifesting as Neteru and the Neteru are the objects of creation, i.e. "nature."

The term Ntr

The Path of Action and Enlightenment

The Great Truths of Neterian Religion

In order to understand the importance of Maat Philosophy not just as a social or secular teaching, it is important to see the interconnectedness of Maat Philosophy with Shetaut Neter spirituality. The fundamental teachings of Shetait Neter reveal the prominent place of Maat Philosophy in the whole scheme of the program of spiritual evolution in Ancient Egyptian mysticism. Therefore, it is appropriate here to present a brief introduction to the basic principles of Shetaut Neter, Ancient African (Qamitan-Egyptian) Religion.

The fundamental principles common to all denominations of Ancient Egyptian Religion may be summed up in four "Great Truths" that are common to all the traditions of Ancient Egyptian Religion.

For more details on the Great Truths and the Fundamental principles of Shetaut Neter see the book *The Book of Shetaut Neter*.

Introduction To MAAT PHILOSOPHY

Maa Ur n Shetaut Neter

"Great Truths of The Shetaut Neter Religion"

I

Pa Neter ua ua Neberdjer m Neteru

"The Neter, the Supreme Being, is One and alone and as Neberdjer, manifesting everywhere and in all things in the form of Gods and Goddesses."

II

an-Maat swy Saui Set s-Khemn

"Lack of righteousness brings fetters to the personality and these fetters cause ignorance of the Divine."

III

s-Uashu s-Nafu n saiu Set

"Devotion to the Divine leads to freedom from the fetters of Set."

IIII

ari Shedy Rekh ab m Maakheru

"The practice of the Shedy disciplines leads to knowing oneself and the Divine. This is called being True of Speech"

Great Truth and Righteousness

"Maa Ur"

"Maa Ur" means "Great Truth."

"Maat"

The word Maa comes from the term "Maat" meaning righteousness, order, and balance. Those who live by the regulations of Maat discover and know truth. Maat is one of the fundamental principles of Shetaut Neter.[2] Maat is a goddess as well as a cosmic principle of order and harmony and a philosophy for attaining that order and harmony that leads to balance and divine peace.

Maat is one of the fundamental principles of Shetaut Neter.[1]

The Maat Goddesses

---

[2] See the books *The 42 Principles of Maat and the Philosophy of Righteousness* and *The Egyptian Book of the Dead* by Muata Ashby

Introduction To MAAT PHILOSOPHY

Who Were the Ancient Egyptians and What is Yoga Philosophy?

The Ancient Egyptian religion (*Shetaut Neter*), language and symbols provide the first "historical" record of Yoga Philosophy and Religious literature. Egyptian Yoga is what has been commonly referred to by Egyptologists as Egyptian "Religion" or "Mythology", but to think of it as just another set of stories or allegories about a long lost civilization is to completely miss the greatest secret of human existence. Yoga, in all of its forms and disciplines of spiritual development, was practiced in Egypt earlier than anywhere else in history. This unique perspective from the highest philosophical system which developed in Africa over seven thousand years ago provides a new way to look at life, religion, the discipline of psychology and the way to spiritual development leading to spiritual Enlightenment. Egyptian mythology, when understood as a system of Yoga (union of the individual soul with the Universal Soul or Supreme Consciousness), gives every individual insight into their own divine nature and also a deeper insight into all religions and Yoga systems.

Diodorus Siculus (Greek Historian) writes in the time of Augustus (first century B.C.):

"Now the Ethiopians, as historians relate, were the first of all men and the proofs of this statement, they say, are manifest. For that they did not come into their land as immigrants from abroad but were the natives of it and so justly bear the name of autochthones (sprung from the soil itself), is, they maintain, conceded by practically all men..."

"They also say that the (early) Egyptians are colonists sent out by the Ethiopians, Asar having been the leader of the colony. For, speaking generally, what is now Egypt, they maintain, was not land, but sea, when in the beginning the universe was being formed; afterwards, however, as the Nile during the times of its inundation carried down the mud from Ethiopia, land was gradually built up from the deposit...And the larger parts of the customs of the Egyptians are, they hold, Ethiopian, the colonists still preserving their ancient manners. For instance, the belief that their kings are Gods, the very special attention which they pay to their burials, and many other matters of a similar nature, are Ethiopian practices, while the shapes of their statues and the forms of their letters are Ethiopian; for of the two kinds of writing which the Egyptians have, that which is known as popular (demotic) is learned by everyone, while that which is called sacred (hieratic), is understood only by the priests of the Egyptians, who learnt it from their Fathers as one of the things which are not divulged, but among the Ethiopians, everyone uses these forms of letters. Furthermore, the orders of the priests, they maintain, have much the same position among both peoples; for all are clean who are engaged in the service of the gods, keeping themselves shaven, like the Ethiopian priests, and having the same dress and form of staff, which is shaped like a plough and is carried by their kings who wear high felt hats which end in a knob in the top and are circled by the serpents which they call asps; and this symbol appears to carry the thought that it will be the lot who shall dare to attack the king to encounter

the (early) Egyptians are colonists sent out by the Ethiopians

The Path of Action and Enlightenment

death-carrying stings. Many other things are told by them concerning their own antiquity and the colony which they sent out that became the Egyptians, but about this there is no special need of our writing anything."

The Ancient Egyptian texts state:

"Our people originated at the base of the mountain of the Moon, at the origin of the Nile river."

"KMT"
"Egypt", "Burnt", "Land of Blackness","Land of the Burnt People."

KMT (Ancient Egypt) is situated close to Lake Victoria in present day Africa. This is the same location where the earliest human remains have been found, in the land currently known as Ethiopia-Tanzania. Recent genetic technology as reported in the new encyclopedias and leading news publications has revealed that all peoples of the world originated in Africa and migrated to other parts of the world prior to the last Ice Age 40,000 years ago. Therefore, as of this time, genetic testing has revealed that all humans are alike. The earliest bone fossils which have been found in many parts of the world were those of the African Grimaldi type. During the Ice Age, it was not possible to communicate or to migrate. Those trapped in specific locations were subject to the regional forces of weather and climate. Less warmer climates required less body pigment, thereby producing lighter pigmented people who now differed from their dark-skinned ancestors. After the Ice Age when travel was possible, these light-skinned people who had lived in the northern, colder regions of harsh weather during the Ice Age period moved back to the warmer climates of their ancestors, and mixed with the people there who had remained dark-skinned, thereby producing the Semitic colored people. "Semite" means mixture of skin color shades.

Therefore, there is only one human race who, due to different climactic and regional exposure, changed to a point where there seemed to be different "types" of people. Differences were noted with respect to skin color, hair texture, customs, languages, and with respect to the essential nature (psychological and emotional makeup) due to the experiences each group had to face and overcome in order to survive.

From a philosophical standpoint, the question as to the origin of humanity is redundant when it is understood that <u>ALL</u> come from one origin which some choose to call the "Big Bang" and others "The Supreme Being."

"Thou makest the color of the skin of one race to be different from that of another, but however many may be the varieties of mankind, it is thou that makes them all to live."
—Ancient Egyptian Proverb from *The Hymns of Amun*

Introduction To MAAT PHILOSOPHY

"Souls, Heru, son, are of the self-same nature, since they came from the same place where the Creator modeled them; nor male nor female are they. Sex is a thing of bodies not of Souls."
—Ancient Egyptian Proverb from *The teachings of Aset to Heru*

Historical evidence proves that Ethiopia-Nubia already had Kingdoms at least 300 years before the first Kingdom-Pharaoh of Egypt.

"Ancient Egypt was a colony of Nubia - Ethiopia. ...Asar having been the leader of the colony..."

"And upon his return to Greece, they gathered around and asked, "tell us about this great land of the Blacks called Ethiopia." And Herodotus said, "There are two great Ethiopian nations, one in Sind (India) and the other in Egypt."

Recorded by Egyptian high priest *Manetho* (300 B.C.)
also Recorded by *Diodorus* (Greek historian 100 B.C.)

The pyramids themselves however, cannot be dated, but indications are that they existed far back in antiquity. The Pyramid Texts (hieroglyphics inscribed on pyramid walls) and Coffin Texts (hieroglyphics inscribed on coffins) speak authoritatively on the constitution of the human spirit, the vital Life Force along the human spinal cord (known in India as *"Kundalini"*), the immortality of the soul, reincarnation and the law of Cause and Effect (known in India as the Law of Karma).

The Path of Action and Enlightenment

What is Yoga Philosophy and Spiritual Practice

Since a complete treatise on the theory and practice of yoga would require several volumes, only a basic outline will be given here.

When we look out upon the world, we are often baffled by the multiplicity which constitutes the human experience. What do we really know about this experience? Many scientific disciplines have developed over the last two hundred years for the purpose of discovering the mysteries of nature, but this search has only engendered new questions about the nature of existence. Yoga is a discipline or way of life designed to promote the physical, mental and spiritual development of the human being. It leads a person to discover the answers to the most important questions of life such as Who am I?, Why am I here? and Where am I going?

The Term Yoga is from Sanskrit-East India. The African term is "Sema." The literal meaning of the word YOGA is to *"YOKE"* or to *"LINK"* back. The implication is: to link back to the original source, the original essence, that which transcends all mental and intellectual attempts at comprehension, but which is the essential nature of everything in CREATION. While in the strict or dogmatic sense, Yoga philosophy and practice is a separate discipline from religion, yoga and religion have been linked at many points throughout history. In a manner of speaking, Yoga as a discipline may be seen as a non-sectarian transpersonal science or practice to promote spiritual development and harmony of mind and body thorough mental and physical disciplines including meditation, psycho-physical exercises, and performing action with the correct attitude.

> The Term Yoga is from Sanskrit-East India. The African term is "Sema."

The disciplines of Yoga fall under five major categories. These are: *Yoga of Wisdom, Yoga of Devotional Love, Yoga of Meditation, Tantric Yoga* and *Yoga of Selfless Action.* Within these categories there are subsidiary forms which are part of the main disciplines. The important point to remember is that all aspects of yoga can and should be used in an integral fashion to effect an efficient and harmonized spiritual movement in the practitioner. Therefore, while there may be an area of special emphasis, other elements are bound to become part of the yoga program as needed. For example, while a yogin may place emphasis on the yoga of wisdom, they may also practice devotional yoga and meditation yoga along with the wisdom studies.

While it is true that yogic practices may be found in religion, strictly speaking, yoga is neither a religion or a philosophy. It should be thought of more as a way of life or discipline for promoting greater fullness and experience of life. Yoga was developed at the dawn of history by those who wanted more out of life. These special men and women wanted to discover the true origins of creation and of themselves. Therefore, they set out to explore the vast reaches of consciousness within themselves. They are sometimes referred to as "Seers", "Sages", etc. Awareness or consciousness can only be increased when the mind is in a state of peace and harmony. Thus, the disciplines of meditation (which are part of Yoga), and wisdom (the philosophical teachings for understanding reality as it is) are the primary means to controlling the mind and allowing the individual to mature psychologically and spiritually.

Introduction To MAAT PHILOSOPHY

The teachings which were practiced in the Ancient Egyptian temples were the same ones later intellectually defined into a literary form by the Indian Sages of Vedanta and Yoga. This was discussed in my book *Egyptian Yoga: The Philosophy of Enlightenment*. The Indian Mysteries of Yoga and Vedanta represent an unfolding and intellectual exposition of the Egyptian Mysteries. Also, the study of Gnostic Christianity or Christianity before Roman Catholicism will be useful to our study since Christianity originated in Ancient Egypt and was also based on the Ancient Egyptian Mysteries. Therefore, the study of the Egyptian Mysteries, early Christianity and Indian Vedanta-Yoga will provide the most comprehensive teaching on how to practice the disciplines of yoga leading to the attainment of Enlightenment.

The question is how to accomplish these seemingly impossible tasks? How to transform yourself and realize the deepest mysteries of existence? How to discover "who am I?" This is the mission of Yoga Philosophy and the purpose of yogic practices. Yoga does not seek to convert or impose religious beliefs on any one. Ancient Egypt was the source of civilization and the source of religion and Yoga. Therefore, all systems of mystical spirituality can coexist harmoniously within these teachings when they are correctly understood.

The goal of yoga is to promote integration of the mind-body-spirit complex in order to produce optimal health of the human being. This is accomplished through mental and physical exercises which promote the free flow of spiritual energy by reducing mental complexes caused by ignorance. There are two roads which human beings can follow, one of wisdom and the other of ignorance. The path of the masses is generally the path of ignorance which leads them into negative situations, thoughts and deeds. These in turn lead to ill health and sorrow in life. The other road is based on wisdom and it leads to health, true happiness and enlightenment.

The goal of yoga is to promote integration of the mind-body-spirit

Our mission is to extol the wisdom of yoga and mystical spirituality from the Ancient Egyptian perspective and to show the practice of the teachings through our books, videos and audio productions. You may find a complete listing of other books by the author in the back of this volume.

The Path of Action and Enlightenment

How to study the wisdom teachings:

There is a specific technique which is prescribed by the scriptures themselves for studying the teachings, proverbs and aphorisms of mystical wisdom. The method is as follows:

The spiritual aspirant should read the desired text thoroughly, taking note of any particular teachings which resonates with him or her. The aspirant should make a habit of collecting those teachings and reading them over frequently. The scriptures should be read and re-read because the subtle levels of the teachings will be increasingly understood the more the teachings are reviewed. One useful exercise is to choose some of the most special teachings you would like to focus on and place them in large type or as posters in your living areas so as to be visible to remind you of the teaching.

The aspirant should discuss those teachings with others of like mind when possible because this will help to promote greater understanding and act as an active spiritual practice in which the teachings are kept at the forefront of the mind. In this way, the teachings can become an integral part of everyday life and not reserved for a particular time of day or of the week.

The study of the wisdom teachings should be a continuous process in which the teachings become the predominant factor of life rather than the useless and oftentimes negative and illusory thoughts of those who are ignorant of spiritual truths. This spiritual discipline should be observed until Enlightenment is attained.

May you discover supreme peace in this very lifetime!

⸺

(HETEP - Supreme Peace)

Introduction to Egyptian Yoga

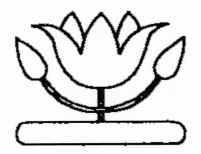

The Path of Action and Enlightenment

What is Yoga and How does Maat Philosophy Relate to Yoga?

Maat Philosophy is an aspect of Yogic Teaching. Therefore it is important to understand Maat Sema (Yoga) in the context of all the Smai Tawi (Egyptian Yoga) traditions. Therefore it is appropriate here to present a brief introduction to the concepts of Yoga and the specific Yogic teachings that developed in Ancient Africa and later in India.

Most students of yoga are familiar with the yogic traditions of India consider that the Indian texts such as the Bhagavad Gita, Mahabharata, Patanjali Yoga Sutras, etc. are the primary and original source of Yogic philosophy and teaching. However, upon examination, the teachings currently espoused in all of the major forms of Indian Yoga can be found in Ancient Egyptian scriptures, inscribed in papyrus and on temple walls as well as steles, statues, obelisks and other sources.

Yoga is the practice of mental, physical and spiritual disciplines which lead to self-control and self-discovery by purifying the mind, body and spirit, so as to discover the deeper spiritual essence which lies within every human being and object in the universe. In essence, the goal of Yoga practice is to unite or *yoke* one's individual consciousness with Universal or Cosmic consciousness. Therefore, Ancient Egyptian religious practice, especially in terms of the rituals and other practices of the Ancient Egyptian Temple system known as *Shetaut Neter* (the way of the hidden Supreme Being), spiritual disciplines were known in Ancient times as *Smai Tawi* "Egyptian Yoga," should as well be considered as universal streams of self-knowledge philosophy which influenced and inspired the great religions and philosophers to this day. In this sense, religion, in its purest form, is also a Yoga system, as it seeks to reunite the soul with its true and original source, God. In broad terms, any spiritual movement or discipline that brings one closer to self-knowledge is a "Yogic" movement. The main recognized forms of Yoga disciplines are:

Yoga is the practice of mental, physical and spiritual disciplines

- *Sema Tawi (Yoga) of Wisdom,*
- *Sema Tawi (Yoga) of Devotional Love,*
- *Sema Tawi (Yoga) of Meditation,*
    - *Physical Postures Yoga*
- *Sema Tawi (Yoga) of Selfless Action,*
- *Sema Tawi (Yoga) of Serpent Power*

The diagram below shows the relationship between the Yoga disciplines and the path of mystical religion (religion practiced in its three complete steps: 1st receiving the myth {knowledge}, 2nd practicing the rituals of the myth {following the teachings of the myth} and 3rd entering into a mystical experience {becoming one with the central figure of the myth}).

Introduction To MAAT PHILOSOPHY

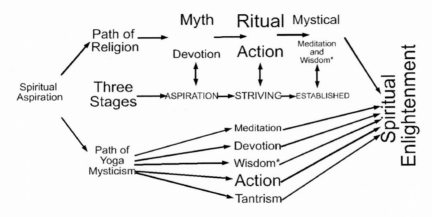

So the disciplines of Yoga fall under five major categories. These are: *Yoga of Wisdom, Yoga of Devotional Love, Yoga of Meditation, Tantric Yoga* and *Yoga of Selfless Action.* When these disciplines are practiced in a harmonized manner this practice is called "Integral Yoga." Within these categories there are subsidiary forms which are part of the main disciplines. The emphasis in the Kamitan Asarian Myth is on the Yoga of Wisdom, Yoga of Devotional Love and Yoga of Selfless Action. The important point to remember is that all aspects of Yoga can and should be used in an integral fashion to effect an efficient and harmonized spiritual movement in the practitioner. Therefore, while there may be an area of special emphasis, other elements are bound to become part of the Yoga program as needed. For example, while a Yogin (practitioner of Yoga, aspirant, initiate) may place emphasis on the Yoga of Wisdom, they may also practice Devotional Yoga and Meditation Yoga along with the wisdom studies. So the practice of any discipline that leads to oneness with Supreme Consciousness can be called Yoga. If you study, rationalize and reflect upon the teachings, you are practicing *Yoga of Wisdom.* If you meditate upon the teachings and your Higher Self, you are practicing *Yoga of Meditation.*

Thus, whether or not you refer to it as such, if you practice rituals which identify you with your spiritual nature, you are practicing *Yoga of Ritual Identification* (which is part of the Yoga of Wisdom {Kamitan-Rekh, Indian-Jnana} and the Yoga of Devotional Love {Kamitan-Ushet, Indian-Bhakti} of the Divine). If you develop your physical nature and psychic energy centers, you are practicing *Serpent Power* (Kamitan-*Uraeus or* Indian-*Kundalini) Yoga* (which is part of Tantric Yoga). If you practice living according to the teachings of ethical behavior and selflessness, you are practicing *Yoga of Action* (Kamitan-Maat, Indian-Karma) in daily life. If you practice turning your attention towards the Divine by developing love for the Divine, then it is called *Devotional Yoga* or *Yoga of Divine Love.* The practitioner of Yoga is called a Yogin (male practitioner) or Yogini (female practitioner), or the term "Yogi" may be used to refer to either a female or male practitioner in general terms. One who has attained the culmination of Yoga (union with the Divine) is also called a Yogi. In this manner, Yoga has been developed into many disciplines which may be used in an integral fashion to achieve the same goal: Enlightenment. Therefore, the aspirant is to learn about all of the paths of Yoga and choose those elements which best suit {his/her} personality or practice them all in an integral, balanced way.

Enlightenment is the term used to describe the highest level of spiritual awakening. It means attaining such a level of spiritual awareness that one discovers the underlying unity of the entire universe as well as the fact that the source of all creation is the same source from which the innermost Self within every human heart arises.

Enlightenment is the term used to describe the highest level of spiritual awakening.

What is Egyptian Yoga?

The Term "Egyptian Yoga" and The Philosophy Behind It

As previously discussed, Yoga in all of its forms were practiced in Egypt apparently earlier than anywhere else in our history. This point of view is supported by the fact that there is documented scriptural and iconographical evidence of the disciplines of virtuous living, dietary purification, study of the wisdom teachings and their practice in daily life, psychophysical and psycho-spiritual exercises and meditation being practiced in Ancient Egypt, long before the evidence of its existence is detected in India (including the Indus Valley Civilization) or any other early civilization (Sumer, Greece, China, etc.).

The teachings of Yoga are at the heart of *Prt m Hru*. As explained earlier, the word "Yoga" is a Sanskrit term meaning to unite the individual with the Cosmic. The term has been used in certain parts of this book for ease of communication since the word "Yoga" has received wide popularity especially in western countries in recent years. The Ancient Egyptian equivalent term to the Sanskrit word yoga is: *"Smai"* or *"Sema." Smai* means union, and the following determinative terms give it a spiritual significance, at once equating it with the term "Yoga" as it is used in India. When used in conjunction with the Ancient Egyptian symbol which means land, *"Ta,"* the term "union of the two lands" arises. The Ancient Egyptians called the disciplines of Yoga in Ancient Egypt by the term *"Smai Tawi."* So what does Smai Tawi mean?

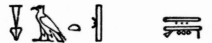

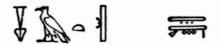

Smai Tawi
(From Chapter 4 of the *Prt m Hru*)

The Ancient Egyptian Symbols of Yoga

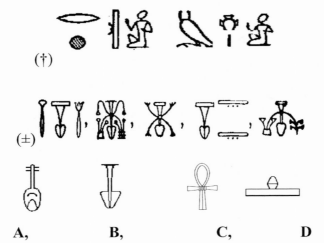

A,   **B,**   **C,**   **D**

The theme of the arrangement of the symbols above is based on the idea that in mythological and philosophic forms, Egyptian mythology and philosophy merge with world mythology, philosophy and religion. The hieroglyphic symbols at the very top (†) mean: ***"Know Thyself," "Self knowledge is the basis of all true knowledge"*** and (±) abbreviated forms of ***Smai taui,*** signifies "Egyptian Yoga." The next four below represent the four words in Egyptian Philosophy, which mean ***"YOGA."*** They are: (A) ***"Nefer"*** (B) ***"Sema"*** (C) ***"Ankh"*** and (D) ***"Hetep."***

The Path of Action and Enlightenment

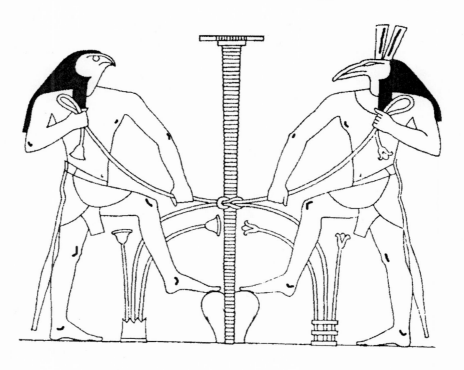

Above left: Smai Heru-Set, Heru and Set join forces to tie up the symbol of Union (Sema —see (B) above). The Sema symbol refers to the Union of Upper Egypt (Lotus) and Lower Egypt (Papyrus) under one ruler, but also at a more subtle level, it refers to the union of one's Higher Self and lower self (Heru and Set), as well as the control of one's breath (Life Force) through the union (control) of the lungs (breathing organs). The character of Heru and Set are an integral part of the Pert Em Heru.

The central and most popular character within Ancient Egyptian Religion of Asar is Heru, who is an incarnation of his father, Asar. Asar is killed by his brother Set who, out of greed and demoniac (Setian) tendency, craved to be the ruler of Egypt. With the help of Djehuti, the God of wisdom, Aset, the great mother and HetHeru, his consort, Heru prevailed in the battle against Set for the rulership of Kemit (Egypt). Heru's struggle symbolizes the struggle of every human being to regain rulership of the Higher Self and to subdue the lower self.

The original name given to these writings by the Ancient Egyptians is *Medu Neter*

The most ancient writings in our historical period are from the Ancient Egyptians. These writings are referred to as hieroglyphics. The original name given to these writings by the Ancient Egyptians is *Medu Neter,* meaning "the writing of God" or *Neter Medu* or "Divine Speech." These writings were inscribed in temples, coffins and papyruses and contained the teachings in reference to the spiritual nature of the human being and the ways to promote spiritual emancipation, awakening or resurrection. The Ancient Egyptian proverbs presented in this text are translations from the original hieroglyphic scriptures. An example of hieroglyphic text was presented above in the form of the text of Smai Taui or "Egyptian Yoga."

Introduction To MAAT PHILOSOPHY

Egyptian Philosophy may be summed up in the following proverbs, which clearly state that the soul is heavenly or divine and that the human being must awaken to the true reality, which is the Spirit, Self.

"Self knowledge is the basis of true knowledge."

"Soul to heaven, body to earth."

"Man is to become God-like through a life of virtue and the cultivation of the spirit
through scientific knowledge, practice and bodily discipline."

"Salvation is accomplished through the efforts of the individual.
There is no mediator between man and {his/her} salvation."

"Salvation is the freeing of the soul from its bodily fetters, becoming a God
through knowledge and wisdom, controlling the forces of the cosmos instead
of being a slave to them, subduing the lower nature and through awakening
the Higher Self, ending the cycle of rebirth
and dwelling with the Neters who direct and control the Great Plan."

Sema Tawi (*Egyptian Yoga*) is a revolutionary new way to understand and practice Ancient Egyptian Mysticism, the Ancient Egyptian mystical religion (*Shetaut Neter*). Egyptian Yoga is what has been commonly referred to by Egyptologists as Egyptian "Religion" or "Mythology," but to think of it as just another set of stories or allegories about a long lost civilization is to completely miss the greatest secret of human existence. What is Yoga? The literal meaning of the word YOGA is to *"YOKE"* or to *"LINK"* back. The implication is to link back individual consciousness to its original source, the original essence: Universal Consciousness. In a broad sense Yoga is any process which helps one to achieve liberation or freedom from the bondage to human pain and spiritual ignorance. So whenever you engage in any activity with the goal of promoting the discovery of your true Self, be it studying the wisdom teachings, exercise, fasting, meditation, breath control, rituals, chanting, prayer, etc., you are practicing yoga. If the goal is to help you to discover your essential nature as one with God or the Supreme Being or Consciousness, then it is Yoga. Yoga, in all of its forms as the disciplines of spiritual development, as practiced in Ancient Egypt earlier than anywhere else in history. The ancient scriptures describe how Asar, the first mythical king of Ancient Egypt, traveled throughout Asia and Europe establishing civilization and the practice of religion. This partially explains why the teachings of mystical spirituality known as Yoga and Vedanta in India are so similar to the teachings of Shetaut Neter (Ancient Egyptian religion - Egyptian Yoga. This unique perspective from the highest philosophical system which developed in Africa over seven thousand years ago provides a new way to look at life, religion, psychology and the way to spiritual development leading to spiritual Enlightenment. So Egyptian Yoga is not merely a philosophy but a discipline for promoting spiritual evolution in a human being, allowing him or her to discover the ultimate truth, supreme peace and utmost joy which lies within the human heart. These are the true worthwhile goals of life. Anything else is settling for less. It would be like a personality who owns vast riches thinking that he is poor and homeless. Every human being has the potential to discover the greatest treasure of all existence if they apply themselves to the study and practice of the teachings of Yoga with the proper guidance. Sema (⚶) is the

The Path of Action and Enlightenment

Ancient Egyptian word and symbol meaning *union or Yoga.* This is the vision of Egyptian Yoga.

The Study of Yoga

When we look out upon the world, we are often baffled by the multiplicity, which constitutes the human experience. What do we really know about this experience? Many scientific disciplines have developed over the last two hundred years for the purpose of discovering the mysteries of nature, but this search has only engendered new questions about the nature of existence. Yoga is a discipline or way of life designed to promote the physical, mental and spiritual development of the human being. It leads a person to discover the answers to the most important questions of life such as, Who am I? Why am I here? Where am I going?

As explained earlier, the literal meaning of the word *Yoga* is to *"Yoke"* or to *"Link"* back, the implication being to link the individual consciousness back to the original source, the original essence, that which transcends all mental and intellectual attempts at comprehension, but which is the essential nature of everything in Creation, termed "Universal Consciousness. While in the strict sense, Yoga may be seen as a separate discipline from religion, yoga and religion have been linked at many points throughout history and continue to be linked even today. In a manner of speaking, Yoga as a discipline may be seen as a non-sectarian transpersonal science or practice to promote spiritual development and harmony of mind and body thorough mental and physical disciplines including meditation, psycho-physical exercises, and performing action with the correct attitude.

The teachings which were practiced in the Ancient Egyptian temples were the same ones later intellectually defined into a literary form by the Indian Sages of Vedanta and Yoga. This was discussed in our book *Egyptian Yoga: The Philosophy of Enlightenment.* The Indian Mysteries of Yoga and Vedanta may therefore be understood as representing an unfolding exposition of the Egyptian Mysteries.

The question is how to accomplish these seemingly impossible tasks? How to transform yourself and realize the deepest mysteries of existence? How to discover "Who am I?" This is the mission of Yoga Philosophy and the purpose of yogic practices. Yoga does not seek to convert or impose religious beliefs on any one. Ancient Egypt was the source of civilization and the source of religion and Yoga. Therefore, all systems of mystical spirituality can coexist harmoniously within these teachings when they are correctly understood.

The goal of yoga

The goal of yoga is to promote integration of the mind-body-spirit complex in order to produce optimal health of the human being. This is accomplished through mental and physical exercises which promote the free flow of spiritual energy by reducing mental complexes caused by ignorance. There are two roads which human beings can follow, one of wisdom and the other of ignorance. The path of the masses is generally the path of ignorance which leads them into negative situations, thoughts and deeds. These in turn lead to ill health and sorrow in life. The other road is based on wisdom and it leads to health, true happiness and enlightenment.

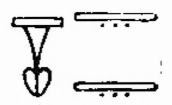

Smai Tawi
(From Chapter 4 of
the *Prt m Hru*)

The Path of Action and Enlightenment

The Sema Tawi of Wisdom

One discipline of Yoga requires special mention here. It is called Wisdom Yoga or the Yoga of Wisdom. In the Temple of Aset (Aset) in Ancient Egypt the Discipline of the Yoga of Wisdom is imparted in three stages:

> 1-<u>Listening</u> to the wisdom teachings on the nature of reality (creation) and the nature of the Self.
> 2-<u>Reflecting</u> on those teachings and incorporating them into daily life.
> 3-<u>Meditating</u> on the meaning of the teachings.

Aset (Aset) was and is recognized as the goddess of wisdom and her temple strongly emphasized and espoused the philosophy of wisdom teaching in order to achieve higher spiritual consciousness. It is important to note here that the teaching which was practiced in the Ancient Egyptian Temple of Aset[3] of **<u>Listening</u>** to, **<u>Reflecting</u>** upon, and **<u>Meditating</u>** upon the teachings is the same process used in Vedanta-Jnana Yoga of India of today. **The Yoga of Wisdom** is a form of Yoga based on insight into the nature of worldly existence and the transcendental Self, thereby transforming one's consciousness through development of the wisdom faculty. Thus, we have here a correlation between Ancient Egypt that matches exactly in its basic factor respects.

THE THREE-FOLD PROCESS OF WISDOM YOGA IN EGYPT:

According to the teachings of *the Ancient Temple of Aset* the Yoga of Wisdom, entails the process of three steps:

Discipline of Wisdom Yoga in Ancient Egypt
1-<u>Listening</u> to the wisdom teachings on the nature of reality (creation) and the nature of the Self.
2-<u>Reflecting</u> on those teachings and incorporating them into daily life.
3-<u>Meditating</u> on the meaning of the teachings.

---

[3] See the book *The Wisdom of* Aset by Dr. Muata Ashby

Temple of Aset
GENERAL DISCIPLINE

Fill the ears, listen attentively- Meh mestchert.

Listening

1- Listening to Wisdom teachings. Having achieved the qualifications of an aspirant, there is a desire to listen to the teachings from a Spiritual Preceptor. There is increasing intellectual understanding of the scriptures and the meaning of truth versus untruth, real versus unreal, temporal versus eternal. The glories of God are expounded and the mystical philosophy behind the myth is given at this stage.

MAUI

"to think, to ponder, to fix attention, concentration"

Reflection

2- Reflection on those teachings that have been listened to and living according to the disciplines enjoined by the teachings is to be practiced until the wisdom teaching is fully understood. Reflection implies discovering, intellectually at first, the oneness behind the multiplicity of the world by engaging in intense inquiry into the nature of one's true Self. Chanting the hekau and divine singing *Hesi,* are also used here.

"Devote yourself to adore God's name."

—Ancient Egyptian Proverb

 *uaa* "Meditation"

Meditation

3- Meditation in Wisdom Yoga is the process of reflection that leads to a state in which the mind is continuously introspective. It means expansion of consciousness culminating in revelation of and identification with the Absolute Self.

Note: It is important to note here that the same teaching which was practiced in ancient Egypt of **Listening** to, **Reflecting** upon, and **Meditating** upon the teachings is the same process used in Vedanta-Jnana Yoga (from India) of today.

The Path of Action and Enlightenment

The Sema Tawi of Right Action

Ari
"Action," "to do something," "things done"

GENERAL DISCIPLINE
In all Temples especially
The Temple of Heru and Edfu

Scripture: Prt M Hru and special scriptures including the Berlin Papyrus and other papyri.

1- Learn Ethics and Law of Cause and Effect-Practice right action
(42 Precepts of Maat)
to purify gross impurities of the personality
Control Body, Speech, Thoughts

2- Practice cultivation of the higher virtues
(selfless-service)
to purify mind and intellect from subtle impurities

3- Devotion to the Divine
See maatian actions as offerings to the Divine

4- Meditation
See oneself as one with Maat, i.e. United with the cosmic order which is the Transcendental Supreme Self.

Plate 1: The Offering of Maat-Symbolizing the Ultimate act of Righteousness (Temple of Seti I)

The Sema Tawi of Divine Love

GENERAL DISCIPLINE
In all Temples

Scripture: Prt M Hru and Temple Inscriptions.

<u>Discipline of Devotion</u>

1– Listening to the myth
      Get to know the Divinity
      Empathize
      Romantisize

2-Ritual about the myth
      Offerings to Divinity – propitiation
      act like divinity
      Chant the name of the Divinity
      Sing praises of the Divinity
      COMMUNE with the Divinity

3– Mysticism
      Melting of the heart
      Dissolve into Divinity

      IDENTIFY-with the Divinity

In the Kamitan teaching of Devotional love:

God is termed *Merri,* "Beloved One"

Love and Be Loved
"That person is beloved by the Lord." PMH, Ch 4

Offering Oneself to God-Surrender to God- Become One with God

Figure 2: The Dua Pose- Upraised arms with palms facing out towards the Divine Image

Sema Tawi of Meditation

The Sema Tawi of Meditation

Sage Amunhotep in meditation

Posture-Sitting With Hands on Thighs

It is well known and commonly accepted that meditation has been practiced in India from ancient times. Therefore, there is no need to site specific references to support that contention. Here we will concentrate on the evidence supporting the existence of the philosophy of meditation in Ancient Egypt.

The Paths of Meditation Practiced in Ancient Egypt

System of Meditation: **Glorious Light System**
Location where it was practiced in ancient times: **Temple of Seti I, City of Waset (Thebes)** [4]

System of Meditation: **Wisdom System**
Location where it was practiced in ancient times: **Temple of Aset – Philae Island, Aswan**

System of Meditation: **Serpent Power System**
Location where it was practiced in ancient times: **Temple of Asar- City of Abdu**

System of Meditation: **Devotional Meditation**
Location where it was practiced in ancient times: **IN ALL TEMPLES- GENERAL DISCIPLINE**

Basic Instructions for the Glorious Light Meditation System- Given in the Tomb of Seti I. (1350 B.C.E.)

Formal meditation in Yoga consists of four basic elements: Posture, Sound (chant-words of power), Visualization, Rhythmic Breathing (calm, steady breath). The instructions, translated from the original hieroglyphic text contain the basic elements for formal meditation.

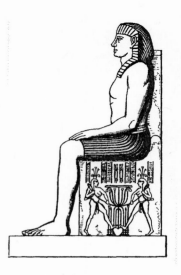

(1)-**Posture and Focus of Attention**
        iuf iri-f ahau maq b-phr nty   hau iu
    body do   make stand, within the Sundisk (circle of Ra)

This means that the aspirant should remain established as if in the center of a circle with a dot in the middle.

---

[4] For More details see the book ***The Glorious Light Meditation System of Ancient Egypt*** by Dr. Muata Ashby.

(2)- Words of power-chant[5]

Nuk Hekau (I am the word* itself)
Nuk Ra Akhu (I am Ra's Glorious Shinning** Spirit)
Nuk Ba Ra (I am the soul of Ra)
Nuk Hekau (I am the God who creates*** through sound)
`
(3)- Visualization

Iuf mi Ra Heru mestu-f n-shry chet
"My body is like Ra's on the day of his birth"

This teaching is what in Indian Vedanta Philosophy is referred to as Ahamgraha Upashama – or visualizing and meditating upon oneself as being one with God. This teaching is the main focus of the Prt m Hru (Book of Enlightenment) text of Ancient Egypt. It is considered as the highest form of meditation practice amongst Indian mystics.[6]

Plate 2: Basic Instructions for the Glorious Light Meditation System- Given in the Tomb of Seti I. (c. 1350 B.C.E.)

As we have seen, the practice of meditation in Ancient Egypt and its instruction to the masses and not just to the priests and priestesses, can be traced to at least 800 years earlier. If the instructions given by sage Seti I and those given by sage Patanjali are compared, many similarities appear.

---

[5] The term "Words of Power" relates to chants and or recitations given for meditation practice. They were used in a similar way to the Hindu "Mantras."
[6] Statement made by Swami Jyotirmayananda in class with his disciples.

Sema Tawi of Postures

The Yogic Postures in Ancient Egypt

Yogic
Postures
were
practiced
in
Ancient
Africa

Most people have heard of the practice of special postures as an east Indian originated discipline. Actually, the system of movements to promote spiritual enlightenment originated in ancient Egypt-Africa more than 10,000 years earlier.

Since their introduction to the West, the exercise system of India known as "Hatha Yoga" has gained much popularity. The disciplines related to the yogic postures and movements were developed in India around the 10th century A.C.E. by a sage named Goraksha.[7] Up to this time, the main practice was simply to adopt the cross-legged meditation posture known as the lotus for the purpose of practicing meditation. The most popular manual on Hatha Yoga is the ***Hatha Yoga-Pradipika ("Light on the Forceful Yoga).*** It was authored by Svatmarama Yogin in mid. 14th century A.C.E.[8]

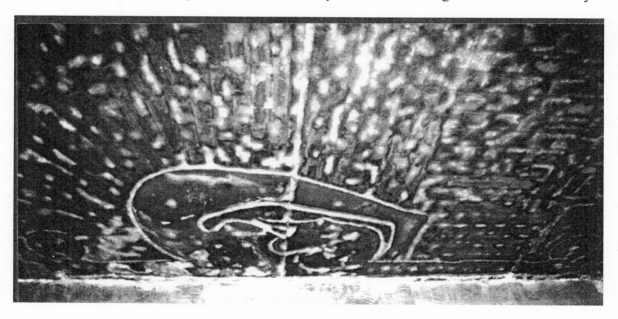

Plate 3: Above- The god Geb in the plough posture engraved on the ceiling of the antechamber to the Asarian Resurrection room of the Temple of HetHeru in Egypt. (photo taken by Ashby). Below: Illustration of the posture engraved on the ceiling.

---

[7] Yoga Journal, {The New Yoga} January/February 2000
[8] ***Hatha-Yoga-Pradipika,*** <u>The Shambhala Encyclopedia of Yoga</u> by Georg Feuerstein, Ph. D.

Introduction To MAAT PHILOSOPHY

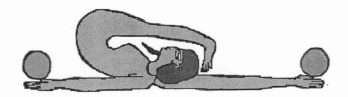

Prior to the emergence of the discipline of the physical movements in India just before 1000 A.C.E.,[9] a series of virtually identical postures to those which were practiced in India can be found in various Ancient Egyptian papyruses and inscribed on the walls and ceilings of the temples. The Ancient Egyptian practice can be dated from 10,000 B.C.E to 300 B.C.E and earlier. Examples: Temple of HetHeru (800-300 B.C.E.), Temple of Heru (800-300 B.C.E.), Tomb of Queen Nefertari (reigned 1,279-1,212 B.C.E.), and various other temples and papyruses from the New Kingdom Era (c. 1,580 B.C.E). In Ancient Egypt the practice of the postures, called *Tjef Sema Paut Neteru* which means "Movements to promote union with the gods and goddesses" or simply *Sema Paut* (Union with the gods and goddesses), were part of the ritual aspect of the spiritual myth, which when practiced, served to harmonize the energies and promote the physical health of the body and direct the mind in a meditative capacity to discover and cultivate divine consciousness. These disciplines are part of a larger process called Sema or *Smai Tawi* (Egyptian Yoga). By acting and moving like the gods and goddesses one can essentially discover one's character, energy and divine agency within one's consciousness, and thereby also become one of their retinue, that is, one with the Divine Self. In modern times, most practitioners of Indian Hatha Yoga see it primarily as a means to attain physical health only. However, even the practice in India had an origin in myth and a mythic component which is today largely ignored by modern practitioners.

Tjef Sema Paut Neteru which means "Movements to promote union with the gods and goddesses"

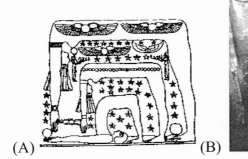

(A)   (B)

---

[9] *The Shambhala Encyclopedia of Yoga* by Georg Feuerstein, Ph. D.

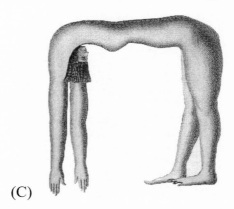

(C)

Figure 3: Above left: The Kamitan goddess Nut and god Geb and the higher planes of existence. Above center and right: The goddess Nut performs the forward bend posture.

The figure above (left) depicts another conceptualization of the Netherworld, which is at the same time the body of Nut in a forward bend yoga exercise posture. The innermost goddess symbolizes the lower heaven where the moon traverses, the physical realm. The middle one symbolizes the course of the sun in its Astral journey. This shows a differentiation between the physical heavens and the Astral plane, as well as time and physical space and Astral time and space, i.e., the concept of different dimensions and levels of consciousness. The outermost symbolizes the causal plane.

Plate 4: Below- The Egyptian Gods and Goddesses act out the Creation through their movements: Forward bend -Nut, Spinal twist -Geb, Journey of Ra – Ra in his boat, and the squatting and standing motions of Nun and Shu.

Figure 4: The varied postures found in the Kamitan papyruses and temple inscriptions.

Figure 5: The practice of the postures is shown in the sequence below.

The Path of Action and Enlightenment

20th Century A.C.E.

1. **Ananda Yoga** (Swami Kriyananda)
2. **Anusara Yoga** (John Friend)
3. **Ashtanga Yoga** (K. Pattabhi)
4. **Ashtanga Yoga** (Pattabhi Jois)
5. **Bikram Yoga** (Bikram Choudhury)
6. **Integral Yoga** (Swami Satchidananda b.
7. **Iyengar Yoga** (B.K.S. Iyengar)
8. **Kripalu Yoga** (Amrit Desai)
9. **Kundalini Yoga** (Yogi Bhajan)
10. **Sivananda Yoga** (Swami Vishnu-devananda)
11. **Svaroopa Yoga** (Rama Berch)

Women first admitted to Hatha Yoga practice

1893 A.C.E.	**World Parliament of Religions – Vedanta Introduced to the West**
1750 A.C.E.	**Shiva Samhita – Hatha Yoga text –melds Vedanta with Hatha**
1539 A.C.E	**Birth of Sikhism**
1350 A.C.E.	**Hatha Yoga Pradipika text -India**
1000 A.C.E.	**Goraksha – Siddha Yogis First Indian Hatha Yoga Practice**
600 A.C.E.	**Birth of Islam**
Year 0	**Birth of Jesus – Christianity**
300 B.C.E.	**Arat, Geb, Nut Egyptian Yoga Postures – Late Period**
1,680 B.C.E.	**Geb, Nut, Ra, Asar, Aset, Sobek Egyptian Yoga Postures – New Kingdom**
2,000 B.C.E.	**Indus Valley – Kundalini – Serpent Power-Lotus Pose**
3,600 B.C.E.	**Nefertem Egyptian Yoga Posture – Old-Middle Kingdom Period**
10,000 B.C.E.	**Serpent Power-Horemakhet Egyptian Yoga Posture – Ancient Egyptian**

The Sema Tawi of Tantrism

> Tantric influence, however, is not limited to India alone, and there is evidence that the precepts of tantrism traveled to various parts of the world, especially Nepal, Tibet, China, Japan and parts of South-East Asia; its influence has also been evident in Mediterranean cultures such as those of Egypt and Crete.[10]
>
> -Ajit Mookerjee (Indian Scholar-Author –from the book *The Tantric Way*)

Tantra Yoga is purported to be the oldest system of Yoga. Tantra Yoga is a system of Yoga which seeks to promote the re-union between the individual and the Absolute Reality, through the worship of nature and ultimately the Cosmos as an expression of the Absolute. Since nature is an expression of GOD, it gives clues as to the underlying reality that sustains it and the way to achieve wisdom, i.e. transcendence of it. The most obvious and important teaching that nature holds is the idea that creation is made up of pairs of opposites: Up-down, here-there, you-me, us-them, hot-cold, male-female, Ying-Yang, etc. The interaction, of these two complementary opposites, we call life and movement.

Insight (wisdom) into the true nature of reality gives us a clue as to the way to realize the oneness of creation within ourselves. By re-uniting the male and female principles in our own bodies and minds, we may reach the oneness that underlies our apparent manifestation as a man or woman. Thus, the term Tantra means to create a bridge between the opposites and in so doing the opposites dissolve, leaving unitary and transcendental consciousness. The union of the male and female principles may be effected by two individuals who worship GOD through GOD's manifestation in each other or by an individual who seeks union with GOD through uniting with his or her male or female spiritual partner. All men and women have both female and male principles within themselves.

In the Egyptian philosophical system, all Neteru or God principles emanate from the one GOD. When these principles are created, they are depicted as having a ***male and female*** principle. All objects and life forms appear in creation as either male or female, but underlying this apparent duality, there is a unity which is rooted in the pure consciousness of oneness, the consciousness of GOD, which underlies and supports all things. To realize this oneness consciously deep inside is the supreme goal.

---

[10] *The Tantric Way* by Ajit Mookerjee and Madhu Khanna

The Path of Action and Enlightenment

In Tantrism, sexual symbolism is used frequently because these are the most powerful images denoting the opposites of Creation and the urge to unify and become whole, for sexuality is the urge for unity and self-discovery albeit limited to physical intercourse by most people. If this force is understood, harnessed and sublimated it will lead to unity of the highest order that is unity with the Divine Self.

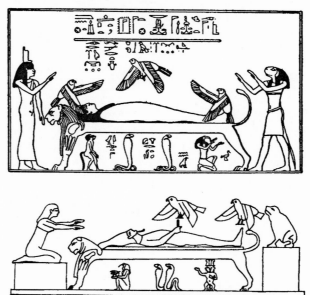

Figure 6: Above- the Kamitan God Geb and the Kamitan Goddess Nut separate after the sexual union that gave birth to the gods and goddesses and Creation. Below: three depictions of the god Asar in tantric union with Aset.

Figure 7: Above-The virgin birth of Heru (The resurrection of Asar - higher, Heru consciousness). Aset in the winged form hovers over the reconstructed penis of dead Asar. Note: Asar uses right hand.

Figure 8: Drawing found in an Ancient Egyptian Building of The Conception of Heru[11]

Aset (representing the physical body-creation) and the dead body of Asar (representing the spirit, that essence which vivifies matter) are shown in symbolic immaculate union (compare to the "Kali Position" on the following page) begetting Heru, symbolizing to the immaculate conception which takes place at the birth of the spiritual life in every human: the birth of the soul (Ba) in a human is the birth of Heru.

-From a Stele at the British Museum 1372. 13th Dyn.

Figure 9: Above- the god Shiva and his consort Shakti

The "Kali position" (above) features **Shiva and Shakti (Kundalini-Prakriti)** in divine union (India). As with Asar and Aset of Egypt, Shiva is the passive, male aspect who "gives" the life essence (spirit) and creative impetus and Shakti is energy, creation, the active aspect of GOD. Thus Creation is akin to the idea of GOD making love with him/herself. Shiva and Shakti are the true essence of the human being, composed of spirit and matter (body). In the active aspect, the female is in the "active" position while the male is in the "passive" position. In Kamitan philosophy, the god Geb is the earth and the goddess Nut is the sky. Just as the earth is sedentary and the sky is dynamic so too are the divinities depicted in this way in Southern (African) and Eastern (India) iconography.

In Kamitan philosophy, the god Geb is the earth and the goddess Nut is the sky.

Figure 10: Above- Buddha and his consort.

---

[11] *Sexual Life in Ancient Egypt* by Lise Manniche

Above: Tibetan Buddhist representation of The Dharmakaya, the cosmic father-mother. expressing the idea of the Supreme Being as a union of both male and female principals.

Notice that the female divinities are always on the top position. This is classic in Eastern and Kamitan mysticism. It is a recognition that the spirit (male aspect) is sedentary while matter, the female aspect, is in perpetual motion and the two complement and complete each other.

Figure 11: Below left- The Triune ithyphallic form of Asar[12]

Figure 12: Below right- the Trilinga (Triune ithyphallic form) of Shiva.[13]

Figure 13: Below far right- the multi-armed (all-pervasive) dancing Shiva-whose dance sustains the Creation.

Figure 14: Below- left Ashokan[14] pillar with lion capital-Kamitan pillar with lion capitals. Center: Ancient Egyptian pillar with lion capitals. Far right: the Ethiopian divinity Apedemak, displaying the same leonine trinity concept and the multi-armed motif.

---

[12] For more details see the book *Egyptian Yoga Volume 1*
[13] For more details see the book *Egyptian Yoga Volume 1*
[14] Constructed in the period of the Indian King Asoka (Ashoka) who adopted Buddhism.

The trinity symbolically relates the nature of the Divine, who is the source and sustenance of the three worlds (physical, astral and causal), the three states of consciousness (conscious, subconscious and unconscious), the three modes of nature (dull, agitated and lucid), the three aspects of human experience (seer, seen and sight), as well as the three stages of initiation (ignorance, aspiration and enlightenment). This triad idea is common to Neterianism, Hinduism and Christianity. The idea of the multi-armed divinity is common in Indian Iconography. However, the depiction above from Ethiopia spiritual iconography shows that it was present in Africa as well.

Figure 15: Below (A)- Line art drawing of the Hindu Lingam-Yoni (Phallus-Vulva) of India and the Crowns of Ancient Egypt.

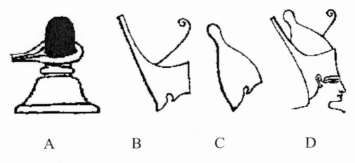

A   B   C   D

Above left, (A)- Line art drawing of the Hindu Lingam-Yoni (Phallus-Vulva) of India symbolizes the unity of the male and female essence into one non-dualistic whole. Figures B-D display the Tantric symbolism embedded in the Ancient Egyptian Pharaonic Crowns. The Red Crown of Lower Egypt, known as the *deshret* crown (B), represents the female principle. The white Crown of Upper Egypt, known as the *hedjet* crown (C), represents the male principle. The Crown of Upper and Lower

The Crown of Upper and Lower Egypt together

Egypt together, known as the *Wereret* crown (D), represent the male principle going into the female- symbolizing unity, balance, and transcendence of duality, i.e. it signifies the attainment of transcendental consciousness as well as rulership over the lower nature and the Higher.   As, no crowns of have survived from ancient times and no references to it have been discovered in the extant records from Ancient Egypt, Egyptologists have speculated on the nature and symbolism of the Pharaonic crowns from the beginning of modern Egyptology up to the present. The understanding of the crowns in light of tantric symbolism has eluded western Egyptologists partly because of the refusal to admit the possibility that there is tantric, yogic, or mystical symbolism and metaphor in Kamitan culture. Therefore, it should be no surprise that the tantric symbolism of the crowns was first noticed in modern times by the Indian scholar Sudhansu Kumar Ray in 1956.[15]

---

[15] Ray, Kumar Sudhansu, *Prehistoric India and Ancient Egypt* 1956

PART I: The Philosophy of Maat
Egyptian Yoga of Action

The Path of Action and Enlightenment

INTRODUCTION TO THE YOGA OF ACTION

The Yoga of Virtue

The American Heritage Dictionary defines *Virtue* as:

> "Moral excellence and righteousness;
> goodness."

What is virtue and where does it come from? Is it something which may be purchased? Is it something that can be cultivated? A person may be ordered to be obedient, to follow rules, etc. Is this virtue? If the ten commandments and so many other laws are established in society, why then is it that there is increasing crime and increasing strife among people? Why is there enmity in the world? Why is there a desire to hurt others? Why is there a desire to misappropriate the property of others?

Anger and hatred cannot be stopped by simply telling someone to be good, loving, forgiving and so on. One cannot become righteous by being ordered to or forced to, no more than a plant can be forced to grow, bear fruit or flowers through a command by the farmer. One can be compelled to follow rules but this does not mean that one is necessarily a virtuous person. Many people do not commit crimes and yet they are not virtuous because they are harboring negative thoughts (violence, hatred, greed, lust, etc.) in their hearts. Virtue is a profound quality which every human being has a potential to discover. However, this requires effort on the part of the individual as well as the correct guidance. Virtue is like a flower which can grow and become beautiful for the whole world to see. However, just as a plant must receive the proper nutrients (soil, water, sunlight, etc.) so too the human heart must receive the proper caring and nurturing in the form of love, wisdom, proper diet, meditation and good will.

Many people are law abiding and peaceful under normal conditions, but if provoked or presented with an opportunity, they will engage in unrighteous activity. Under pressure they may be pushed into stealing, violence or other vices. This is not virtue. The development of virtue in a human being implies that sinful behavior will not be possible even if there is an opportunity for it. True virtue implies a profound understanding of the nature of creation and the heart which will make it impossible to commit crimes or to consider sinful thoughts; as we discover the teachings of Maat, the reasons for this will become clear.

Virtue is the quality which implies harmony with the universe. Virtue is that which leads a human being to come into harmony with the Divine. From a mythological standpoint, sin is to be understood as the absence of wisdom which leads to righteousness and peace and the existence of ignorance which leads to mental unrest and the endless desires of the mind. Sin operates in human life as any movement which works against self-discovery, and virtue is any movement towards discovering the essential truth of the innermost heart. The state of ignorance will end only when the mind develops a higher vision. It must look beyond the illusions of human desire and begin to seek something more substantial and abiding. This is when the aspirant

Virtue is the quality which implies harmony with the universe.

develops an interest in spirituality and the practice of order, correctness, self-improvement and intellectual development. In ancient Egyptian Mythology and mystical philosophy, these qualities are symbolized by the Deities MAAT and Anubis. Maat is the truth and Anubis is the symbol of the discerning intellect which can see right from wrong, good from evil, truth from untruth, etc.

It must be clearly understood that vicious behavior or behaviors that are based on pursuing vices, is/are a factor of spiritual immaturity. Every human being has the innate capacity to develop and experience a virtuous character. Therefore, if one wants to promote peace and non-violence in the world, one must seek to promote virtue in others. This means helping others to discover their inner potential for experiencing a higher state of connectedness to humanity and the universe and a deeper fulfillment in life. Anger and violence are the mark of immaturity. Those who seek to use violence to have their way, to control others, or to promote order in society are in reality expressing their own inability to control themselves. When there is true virtue there will be no desire to control others for egoistic purposes or through the use of violence. A person of strong virtuous character will be able to control himself / herself so as to exercise great care and patience with others. This virtuous development allows a human being to develop a strong will and exert a strong influence on others which can be used to direct them toward what is positive and good. This kind of spiritual power was demonstrated by great Sages and Saints throughout history (Imhotep, Ptahotep, Asar, Aset, Buddha, Jesus, Krishna, etc.). All of the Sages and Saints just mentioned are no different than any other human being who ever existed, except in the lifestyle they chose to live. They chose to live in such a way that the negative in them was eradicated and the wisdom of self-discovery was allowed to blossom. This is the path of virtue wherein life is lived for purifying the mind and body so as to allow the Higher Self, the Spirit in the heart, to emerge and be discovered.

In order to gain this form of spiritual power and spiritual enlightenment, it is necessary to root out every bit of ignorance and negativity in one's entire being. This means that there must be a clear insight into the nature of one's own spiritual innermost nature. This also means that one's actions, thoughts and words must be pure. When the path of virtue is perfected, the heights of spiritual wisdom illuminate the heart. This is the meaning of MAAT Philosophy, Spiritual Enlightenment through the path of Virtue. In the journey of discovering the path of Maat, it is necessary to understand the ancient Egyptian concept of the Judgment.

The Judgment:

"The Conscience (HEART) of a Human is his and her own GOD."

From *the "Book of Coming Forth by Day."*

Religion has three levels: *Mythology, Ritual and Metaphysics or Mystical Philosophy.* The myth of Asar, Aset and Heru represents the *Mythological* level of ancient Egyptian religion. The rituals presented in the ancient *Egyptian Book of Coming Forth By Day* represent the Ritual level. The Philosophy of the Judgment represents the ***Mystical Philosophy*** which is at the heart of ancient religion and is the goal of all spiritual practices. The first two levels are like steps in a ladder and not the end of the road. Those who get lost in the first two levels will not discover the ultimate, transcendental truth behind their religion, but will remain at the level of dogma and empty ritual.

In order to gain a firm grounding for the understanding of Maat and the philosophy of the Judgment, we must first look at the ancient Egyptian Myth of Ra and Asar. Ra is the Supreme Being. He created the universe by emerging from the primeval waters. When he did so he established order in the universe by placing Maat in the place of chaos and confusion. He incarnated himself in his creation by taking on the human form of Asar. Therefore, the soul of Asar is in reality Ra himself. As a metaphor of the human soul, every human being is an incarnation of the Divine Self (God) and suffers the trials and tribulations of human life.

What follows is a compendium of the Asarian Resurrection myth.

A Company of gods and goddesses is a group of deities

The process of creation is explained in the form of a cosmological system for better understanding. Cosmology is a branch of philosophy dealing with the origin, processes, and structure of the universe. Cosmogony is the astrophysical study of the creation and evolution of the universe. Both of these disciplines are inherent facets of Egyptian philosophy through the main religious systems or Companies of the Gods and Goddesses. A Company of gods and goddesses is a group of deities which symbolize a particular cosmic force or principle which emanates from the all-encompassing Supreme Being, from which they have emerged. The Self or Supreme Being manifests creation through the properties and principles represented by the *Pautti* Company of gods and goddesses-cosmic laws of nature. The Company of gods and goddesses of Anu is regarded as the oldest, and forms the basis of the Asarian Trinity.

The Main Characters from the Ausarian Resurrection

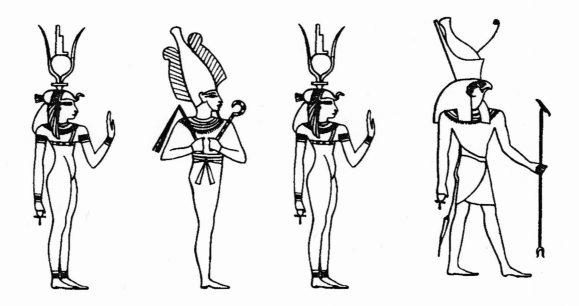

Above from left to right: Isis, Osiris, Nephthys, Horus.

Below from left to right: Anubis, Ra, Tehuti, Hathor.

The Main Characters from the Ausarian Resurrection

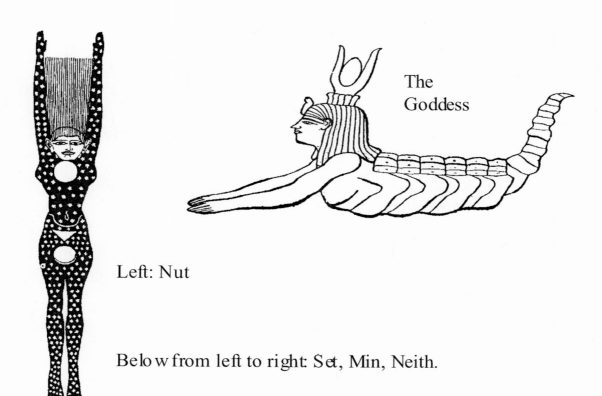

The
Goddess

Left: Nut

Below from left to right: Set, Min, Neith.

Introduction To MAAT PHILOSOPHY

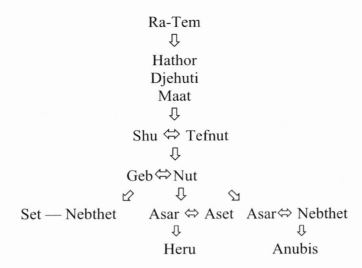

Ra-Tem
⇩
Hathor
Djehuti
Maat
⇩
Shu ⇔ Tefnut
⇩
Geb ⇔ Nut
↗   ⇩   ↘
Set — Nebthet   Asar ⇔ Aset   Asar ⇔ Nebthet
⇩   ⇩
Heru   Anubis

The diagram above shows that *Psedjet* (Ennead), or the creative principles which are embodied in the primordial gods and goddesses of creation, emanated from the Supreme Being. Ra or Ra-Tem arose out of *"Nu,"* the Primeval waters, the hidden essence, and began sailing the *"Boat of Millions of Years"* which included the company of gods and goddesses. On his boat emerged the "Neters" or cosmic principles of creation. The Neters of the Ennead are Ra-Atum, Shu, Tefnut, Geb, Nut, Asar, Aset, Set, and Nebthet. Hathor, Djehuti and Maat represent attributes of the Supreme Being as the very *stuff* or *substratum* which makes up creation. Shu, Tefnut, Geb, Nut, Asar, Aset, Set, and Nebthet represent the principles upon which creation manifests. Anubis is not part of the Ennead. He represents the feature of intellectual discrimination in the Asarian myth. "Sailing" signifies the beginning of motion in creation. Motion implies that events occur in the realm of time and space, thus, the phenomenal universe comes into existence as a mass of moving essence we call the elements. Prior to this motion, there was the primeval state of being without any form and without existence in time or space.

Asar and Aset dedicated themselves to the welfare of humanity and sought to spread civilization throughout the earth, even as far as India and China. During the absence of Asar from his kingdom, his brother Set had no opportunity to make innovations in the state, because Aset was extremely vigilant in governing the country, and always upon her guard and watchful for any irregularity or unrighteousness.

Upon Asar' return from touring the world and carrying the teachings of wisdom abroad, there was merriment and rejoicing throughout the land. However, one day after Asar' return, through his lack of vigilance, became intoxicated and slept with Set's wife, Nebthet. Nebthet, as a result of the union with Asar, begot Anubis.

Set, who represents the personification of evil forces, plotted in jealousy and anger (the blinding passion that prevents forgiveness) to usurp the throne and conspired to kill Asar. Set secretly got the measurements of Asar and constructed a coffin. Through trickery, Set was able to get Asar to "try on" the coffin for size. While Asar was resting in the coffin, Set and his assistants locked it and then dumped it into the Nile river.

Set represents the personification of evil forces

The Path of Action and Enlightenment

The coffin made its way to the coast of Syria where it became embedded in the earth and from it grew a tree with the most pleasant aroma in the form of a DJED or TET. The TET is the symbol of Asar' BACK. It has four horizontal lines in relation to a firmly established, straight column. The DJED column is symbolic of the upper energy centers (chakras) that relate to the levels of consciousness of the Spirit.

The King of Syria was out walking and as he passed by the tree, he immediately fell in love with the pleasant aroma, so he had the tree cut down and brought to his palace. Aset (Auset, Ast), Asar' wife, who is the personification of the life giving, mother force in creation and in all humans, went to Syria in search of Asar. Her search led her to the palace of the Syrian King where she took a job as the nurse of the King's son. Every evening, Aset would put the boy into the "fire" to consume his mortal parts, thereby transforming him to immortality. Fire is symbolic of both physical and mental purification. Most importantly, fire implies wisdom, the light of truth, illumination and energy. Aset, by virtue of her qualities, has the power to bestow immortality through the transformative power of her symbolic essence. Aset then told the king that Asar, her husband, was inside the pillar he had made from the tree. He graciously gave her the pillar (DJED) and she returned with it to Kamit (Kmt, Egypt).

Upon her return to Kmt, Aset went to the papyrus swamps where she lay over Asar' dead body and fanned him with her wings, infusing him with new life. In this manner Aset revived Asar through her power of love and wisdom, and then they united once more. From their union was conceived a son, Heru (Heru), with the assistance of the Gods Thoth (Djehuti) and Amon.

One evening, as Set was hunting in the papyrus swamps, he came upon Aset and Asar. In a rage of passion, he dismembered the body of Asar into several pieces and scattered the pieces throughout the land. In this way, it is Set, the brute force of our bodily impulses and desires that "dismembers" our higher intellect. Instead of oneness and unity, we see multiplicity and separateness which give rise to egoistic (selfish) and violent behavior. The Great Mother, Aset, once again set out to search, now for the pieces of Asar, with the help of Anubis and Nebthet.

Images From The Ausarian Resurrection

The birth of
Horus

Horus and Set in
one personality.

Horus speari ng a hippo potam

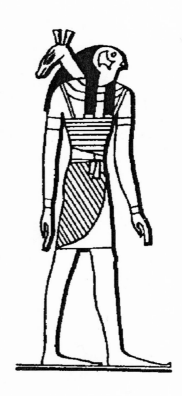

The Path of Action and Enlightenment

After searching all over the world, they found all the pieces of Asar' body, except for his phallus which was eaten by a fish. In Eastern Hindu-Tantra mythology, the God Shiva, who is the equivalent of Asar, also lost his phallus in one story. In Egyptian and Hindu-Tantra mythology, this loss represents seminal retention in order to channel the sexual energy to the higher spiritual centers, thereby transforming it into spiritual energy. Aset, Anubis, and Nebthet re-membered the pieces, all except the phallus which was eaten by the fish. Asar thus regained life in the realm of the dead.

Heru, therefore, was born from the union of the spirit of Asar and the life giving power of Aset (physical nature). Thus, Heru represents the union of spirit and subtle matter, and the renewed life of Asar, his rebirth. When Heru became a young man, Asar returned from the realm of the dead and encouraged him to take up arms (vitality, wisdom, courage, strength of will) and establish truth, justice and righteousness in the world by challenging Set, its current ruler.

The Battle of Heru (Heru) and Set

The battle between Heru and Set took many twists, sometimes one seeming to get the upper hand and sometimes the other, yet neither one gaining a clear advantage in order to decisively win. At one point, Aset tried to help Heru by catching Set, but due to the pity and compassion she felt towards him, she set him free. In a passionate rage, Heru cut off her head and went off by himself in a frustrated state. Even Heru is susceptible to passion which leads to performing deeds that one later regrets. Set found Heru and gouged out Heru's eyes. During this time, Heru was temporarily overpowered by the evil of Set. He became blinded to truth (as signified by the loss of his eyes) and thus, was unable to do battle (act with MAAT) with Set . His power of sight was later restored by Hathor (Goddess of passionate love, desire and fierce power), who also represents the left Eye of Ra. She is the fire spitting, destructive power of light, which dispels the darkness (blindness) of ignorance.

When the conflict resumed, the two contendants went before the court of the Ennead Gods (company of the nine Gods who ruled over creation, headed by Ra). Set, promising to end the fight and restore Heru to the throne, invited Heru to spend the night at his house, but Heru soon found out that Set had evil intentions when he tried to have intercourse with him. The uncontrolled Set also symbolizes unrestricted sexual activity. Therefore, all sexual desires should be pursued in accordance with moral and intellectual principles which dictate rules of propriety that lead to health, and personal, societal and spiritual order (MAAT). Juxtaposed against this aspect of Set (uncontrolled sexual potency and desire) is Heru in the form of ithyphallic (erect phallus) MIN, who represents not only control of sexual desire, but its sublimation as well.* Min symbolizes the power which comes from the sublimation of the sexual energy.* (see *Egyptian Tantra Yoga* by Dr. Muata Ashby)

sexual desires should be pursued in accordance with moral and intellectual principles

Through more treachery and deceit, Set attempted to destroy Heru with the help of the Ennead, by tricking them into believing that Heru was not worthy of the throne. Asar sent a letter pleading with the Ennead to do what is correct. Heru, as the son of Asar, should be the rightful heir to the throne. All but two of them (the Ennead) agreed because Heru, they said, was too young to rule. Asar then sent them a second letter (scroll of papyrus with a message) reminding them that even they cannot escape judgment for their deeds; they will be judged in the end when they have to finally go to the West (abode of the dead).

This signifies that even the Gods cannot escape judgment for their deeds. Since all that exists is only a manifestation of the Absolute Reality which goes beyond time and space, that which is in the realm of time and space (humans, spirits, Gods, Angels, Neters) are all bound by its laws.

Following the receipt of Asar's scroll (letter), Heru was crowned King of Egypt. Set accepted the decision and made peace with Heru. All the Gods rejoiced. Thus ends the legend of Asar, Aset, and Heru.

(For the complete, unabridged version of the Asarian myth and a detailed study of the Asarian Resurrection, including a detailed analysis of the psycho-spiritual symbolism of the characters and events in the epic story, consult the books: *The Asarian Resurrection: The Ancient Egyptian Bible,* and *The Mystical Teachings of The Asarian Resurrection.*

The Mystical Implications of the Asarian Myth for the Study of Maat

The creation itself is based on Maat or cosmic order. Cosmic order is the first requirement necessary in order for human existence to be possible and without human existence the Spirit cannot incarnate into human form in order to experience the physical realities. Secondly, the story shows how Maat leads to peace and order in society. This was evinced by the idyllic life of Asar, who brought order, education and peace to the world. The story also shows how egoism and Setian qualities (anger, hatred, greed, lust, pride, vanity, etc.) lead to death and destruction. Thus, virtuous living, living according to the principles of Maat, engenders life and prosperity, while Setian living leads to sorrow and death.

Setian qualities (anger, hatred, greed, lust, pride, vanity, etc.)

The Ancient *Egyptian Book of Coming Forth By Day* is a ritualization of the Asarian Myth. In it the spiritual aspirant is asked if he or she lived according to the principles of truth and justice while they were alive. If so, they will be worthy of discovering the heights of spiritual evolution. If not they will experience suffering in the astral plane of existence and then they will once again experience reincarnation into a human form.

So every human being experiences a judgment of their character as to whether or not it is in line with Maat which implies growth in spirituality, or with the forces of darkness, ignorance and evil which implies sin and causing pain to self and others. This judgment is the subject of the ancient Egyptian Book of Coming Forth By Day.

The Path of Action and Enlightenment

What is The Pert em Hru?

The Resurrection of Asar and his reincarnation in the form of Heru is a symbol for the resurrection which must occur in the life of every human being. In this manner, the story of the Asarian Trinity, Asar-Aset-Heru, holds hidden teachings, which when understood and properly practiced, will lead to spiritual enlightenment.

The teachings of mystical spirituality are contained in the most ancient writings of Egypt, even those preceding the Dynastic or Pharaohnic period (5,500 B.C.E.-300 B.C.E). All of them contain some portion of the Asarian myth and refer to the religious practitioner (be they male or female) as "The Asar." The most extensive expositions of the philosophy may be found in the writings which have in modern times been referred to as "The Egyptian Book of the Dead."

"The Book of the Dead" was originally known as "Rw Prt M Hrw" or "Ru Pert em Heru" by the ancient Egyptians, which is translated as: "The Utterances for Going Forth into the Light." In Egyptian mythology, Heru (Heru) not only means "Light," but also "Day." Day implies the light of knowledge and spiritual enlightenment as opposed to the darkness of ignorance and human degradation. In fact, Day and Light are two of the most important attributes of the gods Heru and Ra, who represent the the highest potential of every human being. This symbolism is reinforced by the fact that both Heru and Ra utilize the symbol of the Hawk, ⌐, an animal which is swift and possesses sharpness and clarity of vision, and the same symbol of the hawk is used to refer to the human soul. Thus, the text is directed toward enlightening the human soul as to its true nature, allowing one to become aware of his/her deeper Divine essence. Therefore, the title may also read more accurately as "The Book of Coming Forth By Day" or "The Guide for Becoming Heru."

The writings were named "The Egyptian Book of the Dead" by modern Egyptologists. These Egyptologists had obtained them from the modern day dwellers of the area of north-east Africa who had found them buried with the remains of the ancient Egyptian dead. In the interest of simplicity, consistency and accuracy, the name *"Egyptian Book of Coming Forth by Day"* will be used throughout this text. More importantly, with respect to the goal of attaining Enlightenment, the use of title *"Egyptian Book of Coming Forth by Day"* over *"The Egyptian Book of the Dead"* has far reaching psycho-mythological, and hence, psychospiritual implications. The word "Day" represents, light, knowledge and rebirth while the word "Dead" brings images of decay, destruction and finality. In addition, in the ancient Egyptian system of yoga and religion, there is no death, only a transformation based on one's actions, thoughts and innermost consciousness while living in the physical world.

The *Pyramid Texts* and the *Book of Coming Forth By Day* are similar in scripture and purpose. In fact, the origins of the latest versions of the *Book of Coming Forth By Day*, which were composed toward the end of ancient Egyptian civilization, can be traced to the earliest versions. The *Pyramid Texts* are hieroglyphic writings contained in the pyramid tombs of the Kings of the early dynastic period (5,000 B.C.E.). The *Pyramid Texts* and the Books of Coming Forth By Day are collections of utterances and rituals, originally recorded in hieroglyphic scripture and later on in hieratic, demotic and Coptic scripture. They were designed to lead the initiate to transform his/her consciousness from human to divine by purifying the mind with wisdom about

Introduction To MAAT PHILOSOPHY

Pa Neter, or Transcendental Supreme Self, and the neters (divine forces in the universe). Each of these constitute major treatises of ancient Egyptian mystical philosophy and together constitute an advanced, holistic system of spiritual development, comparable to the Yoga-Vedanta philosophy of India. All of these have as their main purpose, to effect the union of the consciousness of the individual human being with the transcendental Self, the Supreme Being.

Over the long period of time (over 5,000 years) of the ancient Egyptian dynastic civilization which lasted over 5,000 years, the teachings presented in the *Book of Coming Forth By Day* evolved from simple principles to a collection of utterances often referred to as chapters or spells. Due to invasions, political conflicts and corruption in the late history of Ancient Egypt, the original teachings became corrupted as they were edited, re-written and added to, by priests and priestesses who were not aware of the original teachings of certain symbols and mystical teachings. Current Egyptological scholarship reckons the total number of chapters or utterances which are to be found in all of the surviving Books of Coming Forth By Day to be 192. However, different papyri contain different amounts of chapters and some contain newly composed chapters. For example, the Turin Papyrus contains only 165 chapters out of the possible 192. So there is no one late version of the *Book of Coming Forth By Day* which contains the entire collection of utterances or which presents them in a completely correct manner as to order or content, though it is possible to trace the teachings given in the earlier times to the utterances presented in the later texts. Some of these later texts, especially those containing chapters 1, 17, 23, 30b, 64, 82, 83, 125, 137a, 174, 175, 177 and 178, along with their vignettes, serve as exegesis (clarification, elucidation) for the earlier texts. The earlier texts, specifically those relating to the founding myth of Asar-Aset-Heru and the Pyramid Texts which constitute the earliest known versions of the rituals of Coming Forth By Day, are the most important sources for deriving the true essence and practice of Shetaut Asar-Aset-Heru.

There is no one late version of the *Book of Coming Forth By Day* which contains the entire collection of utterances

The Path of Action and Enlightenment

Above: The Maati goddesses in the Hall of Judgment.

Maat and The God Djehuti

Forms of Djehuti

Djehuti, Maat and Ra

The god Djehuti is intimately related to the goddess Maat. He is the divinity who was commissioned by Ra, the Supreme Being, to bring the wisdom teachings to the world and establish Maat in the realm of time and space. He is Ra's Mind and heart.

Djehuti is the symbol of right reason, the link to the Higher Self. When the determination to pursue the Divine arises, the struggle becomes a holy war against ignorance and illusion within one's consciousness. If this process is not understood as a struggle to overcome anger, hatred, greed, bigotry, jealousy, etc., within one's self, the energy of the struggle becomes directed to the world outside of oneself in the form of political, religious, social, ethnic, gender, etc., conflicts.

The struggle between Heru and Set does not end with either destroying the other. Heru pursues the path of reason seeking counsel with the wisdom of Djehuti. Wisdom follows the exercise of reason, and reason follows the practice of studying, questioning, reflecting and inquiring into the nature of truth. Set, the lower self, refuses to abide by the decree of wisdom but he is eventually sublimated through his own humiliation and ignorance. In the end, when the aspirant is aligned with all the divine forces, the lower self can no longer struggle. The overwhelming force of the Divine pushes the lower self into a position of service rather than of mastership. This is its rightful place.

The Egyptian *"Book of Coming Forth by Day and Night"* describes the journey of the human soul in the realm of the after life and describes what each man and woman must do to survive death and *"Come Forth"* into the light of *"Day"* (life, illumination, eternal happiness).

At the time of death or prior to death, the heart (consciousness, symbolized by the AB) of the being is weighed against TRUTH, symbolized by the feather of MAAT. Here our godly faculties, symbolized by Anubis and Djehuti and our ability to use them while on earth, are judged.

In the Hall of MAAT, the heart and internal organs of the deceased are judged by 42 judges who are each in charge of one regulation. All 42 regulations or virtuous guidelines for living make up the basis for the 42 "negative confessions." If one lives righteously, one will be able to say that one has <u>NOT</u> committed any offense.

Upon uttering these words, the deceased takes on a new name. Instead of Cathy Jones, she is now Asar Cathy Jones.

If the heart of Asar Cathy Jones is found to be heavier than the feather, instead of joining with Asar, she is sent back to the realm of mental illusion (the world) in the form of an animal or beast to be eaten by the monsters (evil spirits) who feed on sin, greed, un-righteousness, etc.

If the heart of Asar Cathy Jones is found to be lighter than the feather or of equal weight, it signifies that she had led a virtuous life and had mastered the knowledge and wisdom of every God (all of which are aspects of the one GOD), and therefore, she is fit for a new life. Asar Cathy Jones is ready to transcend this world onto the next realm of existence. She is ready to journey back to meet Cosmic Asar who represents Cosmic Consciousness or Ra.

Asar Cathy Jones, through her own virtuous life, is allowed to take or fashion a new, GLORIOUS body, to live in eternity with Asar. Thus, Asar Jones, the individual human soul, meets and joins with Asar, the Supreme Being.

The Path of Action and Enlightenment

This signifies that our own nature is that of universal consciousness. What was separated only by ignorance is now re-united, re-membered. It is only due to ignorance and to distraction in the world of desirable objects that we think we are individual human beings with bodies which are mortal. In reality, we are immortal and eternal beings who are one with the universe and each other.

To realize this even before death, it is necessary to live in a virtuous manner, learning the lessons of human existence and uncovering the veil of ignorance which blinds us from the realization of our essential nature. We must therefore master the knowledge and wisdom of "EVERY" God.

Anpu (God of discernment between reality and illusion) and DJEHUTI (God of Wisdom, experiencing truth) oversee the scales of MAAT. These judge the condition of the Heart (AB) and determine its level of spiritual achievement.

This is also symbolized by the Ammit monster, devourer of hearts, who according to the Greenfield papyrus, determines those who are the advanced spirits and worthy of salvation (those who have developed their higher consciousness centers symbolized by the fourth through seventh rings or levels of consciousness) and those who have not progressed beyond their base animal natures (lower consciousness centers symbolized by the lower three rings). The un-righteous are symbolically devoured by the monsters and evil spirits.

In the Ancient Egyptian as in the Chakra system of India, those who achieve no higher than the level of the third Chakra are considered to be people on the same level of consciousness as animals. Those people will have to reincarnate in order to further evolve beyond this stage. Upon reincarnating, they will once again have the possibility of confronting situations which will afford them the opportunity to perform correct action.

Those people will have to reincarnate in order to further evolve beyond this stage.

Correct feeling and correct thinking lead to "Correct Being" which is the goal --- to "BE" what we really are: ONE WITH GOD.

Introduction To MAAT PHILOSOPHY

The Science Of Virtues

"The Soul is a Prisoner of its own ignorance. In this condition it is fettered with the chains of ignorance to an existence where it has no control over its fate in life. The Purpose of Each Virtue is to Remove One Fetter."

Ancient Egyptian Proverb

Virtues are practiced to promote peace of mind and body: *Hetep.*   Peace of mind promotes study and listening. Study and listening promotes reflection. Reflection on life and the teachings allows the mind to be concentrated:

"making the mind and body still."

Concentration of mind allows meditation to occur. Meditation allows the experiencing of increasing levels of awareness beyond the regular state of waking consciousness, leading to the experiencing of cosmic consciousness: complete freedom.

Practicing the virtues and living a life of simplicity opens the way for spiritual growth by decreasing mental agitation from worries or inordinate worldly concerns. If one maintains balance in all conditions, there will be no situation that will interfere with one's intuition of truth and righteousness, or in achieving mental calmness for meditation. This is the way to the top of the Pyramid.

"Feelings, emotions and passions are good servants but poor masters."

Giving into hate and vengeance will lead to the undoing of the body and spirit. To control one's passions is to master one's own fate. Study the teachings and practice self-control, silence and meditation.

Never go to extremes with anything, for one extreme leads to another. Always strive for balance in all things. Moderation and equanimity in all events and situations are the deeper implications of the scales of *MAAT.* In this manner, the inner peace that allows for the quieting of the mind to occurs. In this quiet, it is possible to discover your deeper Self. This is the meaning of the ancient admonition:

"Now, make thy body still. Meditate that you may know truth."

Ancient Egyptian Proverb

The scales of Maat imply balance, but balance decreed by whom and for what reason?

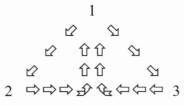

The Path of Action and Enlightenment

From the one: Pure Consciousness, GOD, comes the other two, male and female, so now there can be interaction between the three, which are really one. This principle of duality (male and female) is present throughout all manifestations in the phenomenal world (nature) including the human body. In each of us, there is a male and female aspect of consciousness.

Therefore, in order for creation to exist, the ONE TRUTH must appear to be more than one. Maat is therefore composed of two aspects or two truths, which are really two sides of the same reality. This concept is termed *"MAATI."*

The task of all religious or mystical systems is to BALANCE the interplay between Male and Female (considered together: MAATI), that is, to achieve an internal mode of consciousness which is rooted in the one instead of being caught in the interplay. In other words, *"To keep the balance."*

Evidence from prehistoric times suggests that an imbalance existed between male and female humans such that females controlled the knowledge of birth and therefore controlled men by keeping them ignorant as to their participation in childbirth. Some historians believe that women were able to maintain an illusion of superiority which caused men to hold women in awe. Therefore, women were able to control men and abuse them not unlike the modern day abuse of women by men in our society. As the men gradually became knowledgeable about their participation in conception, they reacted in a vengeful manner. Thus, civilization plunged into the other extreme which eventually led to the witch hunts and other such atrocities.

"Harmony is the Union of Opposites."

Ancient Egyptian Proverb

From a deeper perspective, by having an intuitive understanding of the union underlying creation and of its appearance of duality, one can identify with the Union, the Oneness, and therefore cultivate this unity within one's self. This is the basis of Tantra Yoga --- seeking union with GOD through the worship and understanding of Nature (Female) as a projection of GOD (Male).

"As above, So Below."
"We are created in the IMAGE of GOD."

Ancient Egyptian Proverbs

If we understand that which is below (the physical, manifesting world), then we will understand that which is above (the spiritual world: GOD, who causes the physical world to exist). If we understand the human constitution, we will understand the cosmic constitution, because the manifestation is an exact image of the source. For every function of an organ in the human body and in the objects of the universe, there are likewise cosmic organs and functions which cause them to manifest. Therefore, in order to pursue union with GOD, one must seek to uphold the Cosmic Laws with respect to the balance of the opposites in all areas, through perfect justice, righteousness and with the greatest wisdom which comes not from our mental process, but from our soul (BA). The wisdom of the BA can be accessed through seeking purity of heart and meditation. As we pursue *"the union of opposites,"* we

In order to pursue union with GOD, one must seek to uphold the Cosmic Laws

73

will discover that there are no opposites, only the projected appearance of them. We will discover that underlying the names and forms projected by the Neters (causal powers from GOD), the only reality is GOD. The Cause is GOD, the Causing Neters are GOD, "We are God," All is God. Therefore, from an advanced standpoint we begin to see that there is no cause for the creation of the world, there is no past and no future but only an eternal present. Living life according to the teachings of virtue engenders a movement within the human heart which allows spiritual sensitivity to develop. A person becomes sensitive to a transcendental reality which goes beyond ordinary human perception.

The Path of Action and Enlightenment

A Synopsis of Maat Philosophy Based on Kemetic Texts

Living life in contradiction with truth leads to pain and suffering as well as spiritual ignorance. This is called n-Maat (unrighteousness)

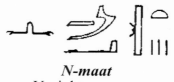

N-maat
Unrighteousness

The Path of Maat: Right Action is the answer:

Ari
"Action," "to do something," "things done"

Arit Maat
Work rightly, lead life of integrity, in accordance with Maatian principles.

Ari em hetep.
Work contentedly, with peace and contentment, without egoistic desire or expectations.

Maat Ab
Thus attain Purity of Heart

Maakheru
Become true of Speech, Spiritually enlightened.

Arit Heru
Receive the Eye of Heru, perfected action, the eucharist, the act of becoming one with the Divine
(the highest action).

PART II: The Art of Virtuous Living and The path of Spiritual Enlightenment Through Maat

Who is Maat?

When Ra emerged in his Barque for the first time and creation came into being, he was standing on the pedestal of Maat. Thus the Creator, Ra, lives by Maat and has established Creation on Maat. Who is Maat? Maat represents the very order which constitutes creation. Therefore, it is said that Ra created the universe by putting Maat in the place of chaos. So creation itself is Maat. Creation without order is chaos. Maat is a profound teaching in reference to the nature of creation and the manner in which human conduct should be cultivated. It refers to a deep understanding of Divinity and the manner in which virtuous qualities can be developed in the human heart so as to come closer to the Divine.

Maat is a philosophy, a spiritual symbol as well as a cosmic energy or force which pervades the entire universe. She is the symbolic embodiment of world order, justice, righteousness, correctness, harmony and peace. She is also known by her headdress composed of a feather of truth. She is a form of the Goddess Aset, who represents wisdom and spiritual awakening through balance and equanimity.

Maat is a philosophy, a spiritual symbol as well as a cosmic energy or force which pervades the entire universe.

In ancient Egypt, the judges and all those connected with the judicial system were initiated into the teachings of MAAT. Thus, those who would discharged the laws and regulations of society were well trained in the ethical and spiritual-mystical values of life (presented in this volume), fairness, justice and the responsibility to serve society in order to promote harmony in society and the possibility for spiritual development in an atmosphere of freedom and peace. For only when there is justice and fairness in society can there be an abiding harmony and peace. Harmony and peace are necessary for the pursuit of true happiness and inner fulfillment in life.

Along with her associates, the goddesses *Shai* (Fortune), *Rennenet* (Destiny) and *Meskhenet*, Maat encompass the teachings of Karma and Reincarnation or the destiny of every individual based on past actions, thoughts and feelings. Thus, they have an important role to play in the Judgment scene of the Book of Coming Forth By Day. Understanding their principles leads the aspirant to become free of the cycle of reincarnation and human suffering and to discover supreme bliss and immortality.

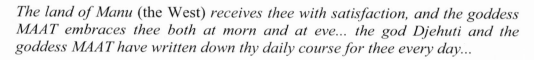

MAAT signifies *that which is straight*. Two of the symbols of MAAT are the ostrich feather (⌡) and the pedestal (⌐) upon which God stands. The Supreme Being, in the form of the God *Ptah,* is often depicted standing on the pedestal.

MAAT is the daughter of Ra, the high God, thus in a hymn to Ra we find:

The land of Manu (the West) *receives thee with satisfaction, and the goddess MAAT embraces thee both at morn and at eve... the god Djehuti and the goddess MAAT have written down thy daily course for thee every day...*

Another Hymn in the Papyrus of Qenna provides deeper insight into MAAT. Qenna says:

I have come to thee, O Lord of the Gods, Temu-Heru-khuti, whom MAAT directeth... Amen-Ra rests upon MAAT... Ra lives by MAAT... Asar carries along the earth in His train by MAAT...

MAAT is the *daughter of Ra,* and she was with him on His celestial barque when he first emerged from the primeval waters along with His company of gods and goddesses. She is also known as the *eye of Ra, lady of heaven, queen of the earth, mistress of the Underworld and the lady of the gods and goddesses.* MAAT also has a dual form or *MAATI.* In her *capacity* of God, MAAT is *Shes MAAT* which means *ceaseless-ness and regularity* of the course of the sun (i.e. the universe). In the form of MAATI, she represents the South and the North which symbolize Upper and Lower Egypt as well as the Higher and Lower Self. MAAT is the personification of justice and righteousness upon which God has created the universe and MAAT is also the essence of God and creation. Therefore, it is MAAT who judges the soul when it arrives in the judgment hall of MAAT. Sometimes MAAT herself becomes the scales upon which the heart of the initiate is judged. MAAT judges the heart (unconscious mind) of the initiate in an attempt to determine to what extent the heart has lived in accordance with MAAT or truth, correctness, reality, genuineness, uprightness, righteousness, justice, steadfastness and the unalterable nature of creation.

Above: The Goddess Maat sits at the bow (in front) of the boat of Ra (Supreme Being). This signifies that she is the one who makes the way, that is, she makes order out of the waves of the primeval ocean as the boat moves. This allows Ra, the spirit, to abide in the forms of the waves, i.e. the forms of creation. Thus, we are to understand that Maat comes first in the spiritual discipline. In other words, virtue must come and then the spirit follows. In other words, the aspirant comes into spiritual enlightenment after purification by practice of Maat Philosophy and its disciplines. When one comes into harmony with the goddess one is actually coming into harmony with the balance of the cosmos and then she (attunement with the cosmic order of the universe) introduces the aspirant to Ra, the Supreme Spirit.

Who is MAATI?

In the segment above we introduced the idea of opposites in creation. The Hall of MAAT known as the hall of judgment for the heart is presided over by two goddesses known as *Maati*. The ancient Egyptian texts reveal that these two goddesses are none other than Aset and Nebthet. They are complementary goddess principles which operate to manifest life-death-life or the cycle of birth-death-rebirth known as reincarnation.

Below: (A and D) The Maati goddesses.
(B) Maat standing.
(C) Maat sitting with eyes closed.

Left: Maati, the two aspects of Maat, also known as Aset and Nebthet.

A

Aset and Nebthet are depicted as looking exactly alike, the only difference being in their head dresses: Aset 𓇋, Nebthet 𓎼 or 𓉠. However, the symbols of these goddesses are in reality just inverted images of each other. The symbol of Aset is the symbol of Nebthet, when inverted 𓇋➔𓉠. Therefore, each is a reflection of the other, thus, it can be said that both life and death are aspects of the same principle.

The Path of Action and Enlightenment

The bodies and facial features of Aset and Nebthet are exactly alike. This likeness which Aset and Nebthet share is important when they are related to Asar. As Asar sits on the throne, he is supported by the two goddesses, Aset and Nebthet. Symbolically, Asar represents the Supreme Soul, the all-encompassing Divinity which transcends time and space. Aset represents wisdom and enlightened consciousness. She is the knower of all words of power and has the power to resurrect Asar and Heru. Nebthet represents temporal consciousness or awareness of time and space. She is related to mortal life and mortal death. Thus, the state of spiritual Enlightenment is being referred to here as Aset, and it is this enlightened state of mind which the initiate in the Asarian Mysteries (*Asar Shetaiu*) has as the goal. The Enlightenment of Asar is the state of consciousness in which one is aware of the transient aspects of creation (Nebthet) as well as the transcendental (Aset). Aset represents the transcendental aspect of matter, that is, matter when seen through the eyes of wisdom rather than through the illusions produced by the ego which can only se Nebthet (gross nature and temporal existence). So, an enlightened personality is endowed with dual consciousness. To become one with Asar Higher Self-Supreme Spirit) means to attain the consciousness of Asar, to become aware of the transcendental, infinite and immortal nature (Aset) while also being aware of the temporal and fleeting human nature (Nebthet).

Aset represents the transcendental aspect of matter

Aset and Nebthet are also known as *Rekhtti:* the two goddesses. They manifest in the Judgment hall of Maat in the *Egyptian Book of Coming Forth By Day* as *Maati* or the double Maat goddesses who watch over the weighing of the heart of the initiate (*The Asar*) in their name as *Rekhtti Merti neb-ti Maati.* Aset and Nebthet are the basis of the judgment of the soul and the criterion which decides its fate in life as well as after death.

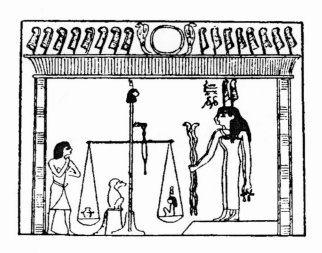

Above: Maati, in the hall of judgement of the conscience of the individual.

Above right- Meskhent seated; Right- Meskhent as birthing block

What is True Virtue?

In order to understand what true virtue is and all of the elements that drive a human being and cause him or her to be the way he or she is, we must begin by understanding the teachings of karma and reincarnation. The human being is not simply a mind and body which will someday cease to exist. In fact, every human being's mind and body are in reality emanations or expressions of their eternal soul. The mind and body are referred to as the ego-personality, and it is this ego-personality which is temporal and mortal. The soul is immortal and perfect while the ego-personality is subject to error, confusion and the consequences of these. If a human being is aware of the deeper soul-reality, this state of being is known as the state of *Enlightenment.* However, if a human being does not have knowledge and experience of their Higher Self, then they exist in a condition of ignorance which will lead to sinful behavior, pain and sorrow in life.

The ego-personality is subject to the forces of time and space and will suffer the consequences of its actions. This is the basis for the teaching of Karma. When the ego-personality dies, the soul moves on. If the human being has discovered his/her Higher Self (purified the heart e.g. mind and body), then the soul moves forward to unite with the supreme Self (God). If the ego in a person is fettered by ignorance, then the soul moves in an astral plane until it finds another ego-personality about to be born again in the world of time and space so that it may have an opportunity to have experiences that will lead it to discover its higher nature. This is the basis for the teaching of reincarnation.

> *"He delivers whom he pleases, even from the Duat (Netherworld)."*
> *"He saves a man or woman from what is*
> *His lot at the dictates of their heart."*

The Path of Action and Enlightenment

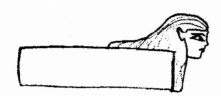

Left: Rennenet and Meskhenet.
From the Judgment Scene of
the Papyrus of Ani.

*Meskhenet, the goddess of the
birthing block, presiding at the
birth of the individual soul.*

The utterances above are directly referring to Meskhenet or karma. Many people believe that karma is equal to fate or destiny, however, this interpretation could not be further from the original understanding of the ancient Sages. The Ancient Egyptian word "ari" means "deeds that follow one." It is equivalent to the intian word "Karma." The etymology of the word, karma, comes from the sanskrit "karman" which means deed or action. In Yoga philosophy, karma also refers to one's actions and these same actions lead to certain experiences and consequences. In ancient Egyptian philosophy, the word Meskhenet comes from the goddess who goes by the same name. She presides over the birth circumstances and life experiences of every individual. She is the one who carries out the decree which has been ordained by Djehuti after the judgment of the heart in the hall of MAAT. It is Djehuti who records the deeds (actions) or karmas of every individual and then decrees what the Shai and Rennenet which are fitting for that particular individual. Then with the help of Shai and Rennenet, Meskhenet causes the individual to experience the proper circumstances based on their previous deeds.

The ancient Egyptian hieroglyphic symbol of the heart is a heart shaped vase, ⚱. The vase is a container which may be used for water, beer, wine, milk, etc. Likewise, the human heart is seen as a vessel which contains thoughts, feelings, desires and unconscious memories. In mystical terms, the heart is a metaphor of the human mind including the conscious, subconscious and unconscious levels. The mind is the reservoir of all of your ideas, convictions and feelings. Therefore, just as these factors direct the path of your life, so too they are the elements which are judged in the Hall of Maati by the two goddesses, Aset and Nebthet, along with Asar. The heart then is the sum total of your experiences, actions and aspirations, your conscience or karma, and these are judged in the balance against the feather of Maat.

Thus, karma should be thought of as the total effect of a person's actions and conduct during the successive phases of His/her existence. But how does this effect operate? How do the past actions affect the present and the future? Your experiences from the present life or from previous lifetimes cause unconscious impressions which stay with the Soul even after death. These unconscious impressions are what constitute the emerging thoughts, desires, and aspirations of every individual. These impressions are not exactly like memories, however, they work like memories. For example, if you had a fear in a previous lifetime or the childhood of your present lifetime, you may not remember the event that caused the fear, but you may experience certain phobias when you come into contact with certain objects or certain people. These feelings are caused by the unconscious impressions which are coming up to the surface of the conscious mind. It is this conglomerate of unconscious impressions which are "judged" in the Hall of MAAT and determine where the soul will go to next in the spiritual journey toward evolution or devolution, also known as the cycle of birth and death or reincarnation, as well as the experiences of heaven or hell. The following segment from the ancient Egyptian "Instruction to Mer-ka-Ré" explains this point.

> *"You know that they are not merciful the day when they judge the miserable one..... Do not count on the passage of the years; they consider a lifetime as but an hour. After death man remains in existence and His acts accumulate beside him. Life in the other world is eternal, but he who arrives without sin before the Judge of the Dead, he will be there as a Neter and he will walk freely as do the masters of eternity."*

The reference above to "His acts accumulate beside him" alludes to the unconscious impressions which are formed as a result of one's actions while still alive. These impressions can be either positive or negative. Positive impressions are developed through positive actions by living a life of righteousness (MAAT) and virtue. This implies living according to the precepts of mystical wisdom or being a follower of Heru (*Shemsu Hor*) and Aset. These actions draw one closer to harmony and peace, thus paving the way to discover the Self within. The negative impressions are developed through sinful actions. They are related to mental agitation, disharmony and restlessness. This implies acts based on anger, fear, desire, greed, depression, gloom, etc. These actions draw one into the outer world of human desires. They distract the mind and do not allow the intellect (Saa) to function. Thus, existence at this level is closer to an animal, being based on animal instincts and desires of the body (selfishness), rather than to a spiritually mature human being, being based on reason, selflessness, compassion, etc.

"His acts accumulate beside him"

(Purification of the heart)

How then is it possible to eradicate negative karmic impressions and to develop positive ones? The answer lies in your understanding of the wisdom teachings and your practice of them. When you study the teachings and live according to them, your mind undergoes a transformation at all levels. This transformation is the "purification of heart" so often spoken about throughout the *Egyptian Book of Coming Forth By Day*. It signifies an eradication of negative impressions, which renders the mind pure

The Path of Action and Enlightenment

and subtle. When the mind is rendered subtle, then spiritual realization is possible. This discipline of purifying the heart by living according to the teachings is known as the Yoga of Action or MAAT.

The philosophy of MAAT is a profound teaching which encompasses the fabric of creation as well as a highly effective system of spiritual discipline. In creation stories, God (Neter Neteru) is said to have established creation upon MAAT. Consequently it follows that MAAT is the orderly flow of energy which maintains the universe. Further, MAAT is the regularity which governs the massive planetary and solar systems as well as the growth of a blade of grass and a human cell. This natural process represents the flow of creation wherein there is constant movement and a balancing of opposites (up-down, hot-cold, here-there, you-me, etc.).

Most people act out of the different forces which are coursing through them at the time. These may be hunger, lust, fear, hatred, anger, elation, etc. They have no control over these because they have not understood that their true essence is in reality separate from their thoughts and emotions. They have *identified* with their thoughts and therefore are led to the consequences of those thoughts and the deeds they engender. You, as an aspirant, having developed a higher level of spiritual sensitivity, are now aware that you have a choice in the thoughts you think and the actions you perform. You can choose whether to act in ways that are in harmony with MAAT or those that are disharmonious. You have now studied the words of wisdom and must now look beyond the level of ritual worship of the Divine to the realm of practice and experience of the Divine.

In ordinary human life, those who have not achieved the state of Enlightenment (the masses in society at large) perceive nature as a conglomeration of forces which are unpredictable and in need of control. However, as spiritual sensitivity matures, the aspirant realizes that what once appeared to be chaotic is in reality the Divine Plan of the Supreme Being in the process of unfoldment. When this state of consciousness is attained, the aspirant realizes that there is an underlying order in nature which can only be perceived with spiritual eyes.

The various injunctions of MAAT are for the purpose of keeping order in society among ordinary people, people without psychological maturity and, or spiritual sensitivity, meaning that they lack an awareness of spiritual principles and moral - ethical development. Also, they provide insight into the order of creation and a pathway or spiritual discipline, which when followed, will lead the aspirant to come into harmony with the cosmic order. When the individual attunes his or her own sense of order and balance with the cosmic order, a spontaneous unity occurs between the individual and the cosmos, and the principles of MAAT, rather than being a blind set of rules which we must strive to follow, become a part of one's inner character and proceed from one in a spontaneous manner.

deeper understanding of cosmic order

This means that through the deeper understanding of cosmic order and by the practice of living in harmony with that order, the individual will lead him or herself to mental and spiritual peace and harmony. It is this peace and harmony which allows the lake of the mind to become a clear mirror in which the individual soul is able to realize its oneness with the Universal Soul.

Introduction To MAAT PHILOSOPHY

The Concept of Action and Fate in Maat Philosophy

Ari

"Action," "to do something," "things done"

Maat Philosophy is based on the concept of "actions." Actions are called "Ari." Ones actions leave impressions of the unconscious mind and these emerge later as desires which impel the personality to certain situations. This concept is illustrated most succinctly in the teachings of Merikara.

In the Kamitan system the god Asar serves the function of administering Maat. The gods base their decisions about one's fate by means of examining one's record as a human being. This record is termed "Karma" in India and "Ari" in Ancient Egypt. In Indian history, the word "Karma" appears in the Vedic tradition with the meaning of the act of sacrifice as in a ritual. In the Upanishadic tradition the word takes on the much more expanded and profound meaning that it has come to represent in modern times, as the "residue or mental impression of any action performed by an unenlightened person."[16] This residue remains with a person even after death due to that person's desire to experience pleasure from their performance of the action, because of spiritual ignorance. Since mystical philosophy maintains that happiness can only come from self-knowledge (Cosmic or Divine Consciousness) and not from worldly pursuits, all egoistic actions will inevitably lead to disappointment, if not in this lifetime, in a future one. However, this is not realized by people because when some actions are performed, they seem to give the desired result of pleasure. This then leads to the developing of craving in the personality as people become dependent on the result of their actions to experience happiness, or as it is referred to in Yoga, "the fruits" of action. The person feels that if they can engage in this action again and again, they will be a happier person or at least derive the same or more pleasure. Thus they strive to perform those actions that seem to bring them pleasure as much as possible, and strive to avoid and consequently they develop dislike for those actions or situations which they perceive as being an obstacle for their experience of pleasure. Many times, their actions to recapture the pleasure that they experienced previously in similar circumstances do not bring them the pleasure that they want due to many obstacles that develop in life, however, people simply make excuses for these times of disappointment or frustration, and continue on with their next pursuit. Another problem is that one cannot pursue that which gives pleasure on a continuous basis. Thus, this is not true happiness. True happiness is defined as an experience of the state of Enlightenment, whereby one experiences joy all the time, in all conditions and circumstances.

This means that true happiness is not a by-product of or dependent on doing some ⌐ true happiness is not... activity or acquiring some object or situation, but rather, it is a state of being. It is unaffected by any situation or circumstance in the world. It is a person's true essence. When an enlightened person performs actions, they are not doing so to become happy as a result, but because it is righteous action that they are being guided to do by their connection to the Divine...thus, in effect, they are performing divinely ordained

---

[16] *A Concise Encyclopedia of Hinduism,* by Klaus K. Klostermaier

works. Thus, karma impels a person to reincarnate in order to attempt the fulfillment of the desire left over from the previous karma, and this cycle of birth, death, birth continues until there is full self-knowledge of the illusoriness of desires, worldly attainments and actions. Thus, karma is not fate but the tendency that a person sets up, in their deep unconscious to like or dislike and desire or repudiate. This duality keeps the mind flowing from adversity to prosperity or from pleasurable to painful situations without achieving a resolution or peace, indefinitely. The same philosophy of the "residue" of action that remains in the mind of a person (deep unconscious level) may be seen in the Kamitan teachings of Meri-ka-ra.

Many people think of the philosophy of Karma as a concept that originated in India. The following text shows that it is a concept that was well understood in Kamit and is very much in harmony with what is today referred to as Karma. In Ancient Egypt the word for karma was Ari, meaning "action" which attaches to a person and leads them to their fate even beyond death. This is the same understanding in Hindu philosophy. The Kamitan teachings to Merikara and the *Pert M Hru* illuminate this teaching in detail. *(Highlighted text is by Ashby)*

Instructions of Merikara

(14) The Court that judges the wretch,
You know they are not lenient,
On the day of judging the miserable,
In the hour of doing their task.
It is painful when the accuser has knowledge,
Do not trust in length of years,
They view a lifetime in an hour!
When a man remains over after death,
*His **Ari (deeds, actions) are set beside him as treasure**,*
And being yonder lasts forever.
A fool is who does what they reprove!
He who reaches them without having done wrong
 Will exist there like a god,
Free-striding like the lords forever!

— Instructions of Merikara Ancient Egypt

a person is the author of {his/her} own fate,

The writings of Merikara confirm the understanding of a subtle aspect of action which follows one after death. This "residue" is judged and the destiny is administered thereby. This signifies that a person is the author of {his/her} own fate, i.e. karmic fortune. This teaching also conveys the relativity of time and space, as the "judges" exist in a different plane than the worldly, physical state and the passage of time is different for them. Thus, this passage also contains a reference which shows a comprehension of the relativity of time in different planes of existence, much like the Hindu metaphysics.[17]

---

[17] *Mysticism of the Mahabharata* by Swami Jyotirmayananda

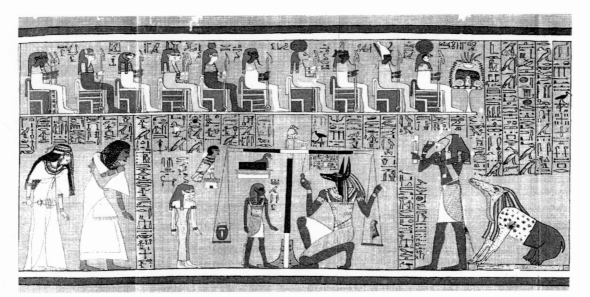

Above- Vignette from Chapter 33 of Papyrus Ani: The Judgment scene from the *Pert m Heru* Text of Ancient Egypt.

Ani and his wife enter the judgment hall. Left to Right: Meskhenet and Rennenet, The Ba (the soul, as human-headed hawk), Shai (standing), Meskhenet (again-this time as birthing block {above Shai}), Anpu, Djehuti, Ammit.

The Judgment scene above shows how a person's own actions are judged and how this leads a person to their fate, either to move on and discover the Divine and become one with the Divine or to suffer due to negative actions of the past or to reincarnate. The Papyrus of Ani dates back to the 18th Dynasty of the Dynastic Period in Ancient Egypt (1500 B.C.E.). It denotes a philosophy related to the Asarian Resurrection theology that has been traced back to the Pre-Dynastic Age and which constitutes one of the central teachings of Ancient Egyptian religion, the Maat principle. The following detailed description of the Ancient Egyptian Judgment scene, alluded to by S. M El Mansouri (above), provides deeper insight into the workings of the Kamitan system of Ari.

Judgment of the Soul. Text: Ani addresses his heart. At top, the gods and goddesses presiding are (right to left: Ra, Atum, Shu, Tefnut, Geb, Nut, Nebethet and Aset, Heru Ur, Hetheru, Saa and Hu (Divine Taste). Far left, Ani enters the hall of Judgment. His heart (conscience) is being weighed by Anpu (Anubis) while the Divine principals Shai, Rennenet and Meskhenet look on. Ani's soul and his destiny also look on while Anubis measures Ani's heart (unconscious mind containing the impressions or "residues") against the feather of Maat (i.e. the principles of the 42 precepts of Maat…truth, righteousness, etc.). At far right Djehuti records the result while the Ammit monster, the Devourer of the unjust, awaits the answer. The hands of Djehuti (God of Reason) are "Shai" which means "destiny" and "Rennenet" which means "Fortune and Harvest." The implication is that we reap (harvest) the result of our state of mind (heart). Our state of mind, including our subconscious feelings and desires, is weighed against cosmic order, Maat. If found to be at peace (Hetep) and therefore in accord with cosmic order (Maat) it will be allowed to join with the cosmos (Asar). Otherwise it will suffer the fate as dictated by its own contents (mental state of unrest

that we reap (harvest) the result of our state of mind (heart) due to lingering desires), which will lead it to Ammit who will devour the ego-personality. That soul will experience torments from demons until it learns its lessons through the process of trial and error, and then pursues an authentic process of mystical practice to become strong enough through wisdom to know itself (become Enlightened). Demons may be understood as negative cosmic energies which it has allowed itself to indulge in, in the form of mental anguish and torments people put themselves through, due to their own ignorance. Self-torment may be regret over some action or inaction while alive or a reluctance to leave the physical realm because of a lingering desire to experience more earthly pleasure. Therefore, one controls one's own fate according to one's own level of wisdom or reasoning capacity.[18]

MAAT as the Spiritual Path of Righteous Action

MAAT is equivalent to the Chinese concept of the *Tao* or *"The Way"* of nature. This *"Way"* of nature, from the *Tao-te-Ching*, the main text of Taoism, represents the harmony of human and Divine (universal) consciousness. Also, MAAT may be likened with the Indian idea of *Dharma* or the ethical values of life and the teachings related to *Karma Yoga,* the yogic spiritual discipline which emphasizes selfless service and the attitude that actions are being performed by God who is working through you instead of your personal ego-self. God is working through you to serve humanity, which is also essentially God. All Buddhist Monks utter the prayer *I go to the Buddha for refuge. I go to the Dharma for refuge. I go to the monastic order for refuge.*

The Buddhist aspirant is admonished to take refuge in the *Buddha* (one's innate *Buddha Consciousness*), the *Dharma*, and the *Sanga* (company of enlightened personalities). The following statement from chapter 9 of the Bhagavad Gita shows how Lord Krishna admonished his followers to seek sanctuary in him as Jesus did hundreds of years later.

<blockquote>32. O Arjuna, those who take refuge in Me</blockquote>

Jesus also exhorted his followers to bring him their troubles "and He will give them rest." Dharma is understood as the spiritual discipline based on righteousness, order and truth which sustains the universe. In the same way, the ancient Egyptian Initiate was to lean upon MAAT in order to purify his or her heart so as to uncover the virtuous character which leads to Divine awareness.

<blockquote>"There are two roads traveled by humankind, those who seek to live MAAT, and those who seek to satisfy their animal passions."

Ancient Egyptian Proverb</blockquote>

It is important here to gain a deeper understanding of what is meant by *action.* In primeval times, before creation, the primordial ocean existed in complete peace and rest. When that ocean was agitated with the first thought of God, the first *act* was

---

[18] *The Ancient Egyptian Book of the Dead* by Dr. Muata Ashby 2000

performed. Through the subsequent *acts of mind* or *efforts of divine thought,* creation unfolded in the form of the various gods and goddesses who form the "companies of Gods." They represent the qualities of nature (hot-cold, wet-dry, etc.) in the form of pairs of opposites. When the first primeval thought emerged from the primeval ocean of pure potentiality, immediately there was something other than the single primordial essence. Now there is a being who is looking and perceiving the rest of the primordial essence. This is the origin of duality in the world of time and space and the triad of human consciousness. Instead of there being one entity, there appears to be two. The perception instrument, the mind and senses, is the third factor which comprises the triad. Therefore, while you consider yourself to be an individual, you are in reality one element in a triad which all together comprise the content of your human experiences. There is a perceiver (the real you), that which is being perceived (the object) and the act of perception itself (through the mind and senses).

With this first primordial act, God set into motion events which operate according to regular and ceaseless motion or action. This is the foundation upon which the universe is created and it emerges from the mind of God. Therefore, if one is able to think and act according to the way in which God thinks and acts, then there will be oneness with God. Human beings are like sparks of divine consciousness, and as such, are endowed with free will to act in any given way. This free will, when dictated by the egoism of the individual mind, causes individual human beings to feel separate from God. This delusion of the mind leads it to develop ideas related to its own feelings and desires. These egoistic feelings and desires lead to the performance of egoistic acts in an effort to satisfy those perceived needs and desires. This pursuit of fulfillment of desires in the relative world of the mind and senses leads the soul to experience pain, sorrow and frustration, because these can never be 100% satisfied. Frustration leads to more actions in search of fulfillment.

The fleeting feelings which most people have associated with happiness and passion are only ephemeral glimpses of the true happiness and peace which can be experienced if the source of true fulfillment within you was to be discovered. MAAT shows a way out of the pain and sorrow of human existence and leads you to discover Asar within you, the source of eternal bliss and supreme peace. If you choose to act according to your own will (ego), then you will be in contradiction with MAAT. This means that you are contradicting your own conscience, creating negative impressions which will become lodged in the heart (unconscious mind) and will cause continuous mental agitation while you are alive and hellish experiences for yourself after death. The negative impressions rise up at given times in the form of uncontrolled desires, cravings, unrest, and the other forms of self-torment with which human life abounds.

How we contradict our own conscience

It is important to understand that when the soul is attuned to a physical body, mind and senses, the experiences occur through these. Thus, the experiences of pleasure and pain are regulated by how much the body, mind and senses can take. If there is too much pain the body faints. When there is too much pleasure the mind and senses become weakened and swoons into unconsciousness or sleep. If there is too much pleasure, there develops elation and the soul is carried off with the illusion of pleasure, which creates a longing and craving for more and more in an endless search for fulfillment.

The Path of Action and Enlightenment

However, after death, there is no safety valve as it were. Under these conditions the soul will have the possibility of experiencing boundless amounts of pleasure or pain according to its karmic basis. This is what is called heaven and hell, respectively. Therefore, if you have lived a balanced life (MAAT), then you will not have the possibility of experiencing heaven or hell. Rather, you will retain presence of mind and will not fall into the delusion of ignorance. Therefore, the rewards of developing a balanced mind during life continues after death. This mental equanimity allows you to see the difference between the truth and the illusions of the mind and senses, in life as well as in death.

Thus, if you choose to act in accordance with MAAT, you will be in a position to transcend the egoistic illusions of the mind and thereby become free from the vicious cycle of actions which keep the mind tied to its illusory feelings and desires. When the mind is freed from the "vicious cycle," the soul's bondage to the world of time and space is dissolved because it is not being controlled by the mind but has become the controller of the mind. When the practice of MAAT is perfected, the mind becomes calm. When this occurs, the ocean of consciousness which was buffeted by the stormy winds of thoughts, anxieties, worries and desires, becomes calm. This calmness allows the soul to cease its identification with the thoughts of the mind and to behold its true nature as a separate entity from the mind, senses, feelings and thoughts of the ego-self. The soul is now free to expand its vision beyond the constrictive pettiness of human desires and mental agitation, in order to behold the expansion of the inner Self.

Actions are the basis upon which the Cosmic Plan of creation unfolds. In human life, it is the present action which leads to the results that follow at some point in the future, in this life or in another lifetime. Therefore, if you are in a prosperous situation today or an adverse one, it is because of actions you performed in the past. Thus, both situations, good or bad, should be endured with a sense of personal responsibility and equanimity of mind (MAAT). From a transcendental point of view, the Soul looks at all situations equally. This is because the Soul knows itself to be immortal and eternal, and untouched by the events of human existence which it has witnessed for countless lifetimes. It is the ego, which is transient, that looks on life situations as pressing and real and therefore either tries to hold onto situations which it considers to be "good" or to get away from or eradicate situations which it considers to be "bad." All situations, whether they are considered to be good or bad by the ego, will eventually pass on, so we should try to view them as clouds which inevitably pass on, no matter how terrible or how wonderful they may seem to be. When life is lived in this manner, the mind develops a stream of peace which rises above elation and depression, prosperity and adversity. By looking at situations with equal vision and doing your best regardless of the circumstances, you are able to discover an unalterable balance within yourself. This is MAAT, the underlying order and truth behind the apparent chaos and disorder in the phenomenal world. In doing this, you are able to attune your mind to the cosmic mind of the innermost Self which exists at that transcendental level of peace all the time.

This means that if you are, deep down, indeed the Universal Self, one with God, and if you have come to your current situation in life of bondage to the world of time and space due to your own state of mental ignorance, then it follows that if you undertake certain disciplines of knowledge (studying the teachings) and daily practice

The Soul looks at all situations equally.

Introduction To MAAT PHILOSOPHY

(following the teachings), those same actions will lead you to liberation from the state of bondage. Ignorance of your true Self is the root cause of your bondage to the karmic cycle of life-death-reincarnation — life-death-reincarnation, etc.

Actions must be performed by everyone. Even breathing is an action. Therefore, nobody can escape actions. No one can say: "I will go far away from civilization and escape all actions and then my actions will not lead me to a state of ignorance about my true Self." This form of thinking is a fallacy because, as just discussed, breathing, eating, drinking, sleeping, sitting, and walking are actions. The process of liberation requires more than just removing yourself from the field of physical actions. You could go to a quiet cave, temple or church and you would still be plagued by the unruly thoughts of the mind which cause distraction from the Self. Thoughts are subtle forms of actions. Therefore, an action performed in thought can be equally significant and cause as much karmic entanglement as an action performed with the body. An action first originates in the mental field (astral plane) of consciousness which is stirred by desires rising from the unconscious mind. This agitation prompts the mind toward thoughts and actions in an attempt to fulfill the desires of the unconscious, but those actions and thoughts create more desires and more future agitation. This is the state of bondage which is experienced by most people and it continues for lifetimes without end. This cycle continues until there is a discovery that desires cannot be fulfilled in this manner. Therefore, the root of desire, ignorance, must be eradicated in order to end the desires of the mind and achieve true peace and balance.

You need to develop subtlety of intellect and profound insight into the nature of the universe and of your innermost Self. The best way to achieve this goal is to practice a blending of wisdom and action in your personal spiritual discipline in order to harmonize your mental and physical qualities.

In this process, you must understand that the ancient Sages have given guidelines for which thoughts and actions are in line with the scales of MAAT, and which actions and thoughts are not. The 42 precepts of MAAT constitute the focus of the Egyptian Book of Coming Forth By Day, however, throughout the book, many injunctions are given. Their purpose is to cleanse the heart of the aspirant.

> *"The wise person who acts with MAAT is free of falsehood and disorder."*
>
> Ancient Egyptian Proverb

The practice of MAAT signifies *wisdom in action.* This is to say that the teachings are to be practiced in ordinary day to day situations, and when the deeper implications of this practice are understood, one will be led to purity in action and thought.

In order to become one with the Divine, you must become the Divine in thought and deed. This means that you must spiritualize your actions and your thoughts at all times and under all conditions. Actions which present themselves to you in the normal course of the day, as well as those actions which you have planned for the future, should be evaluated by your growing intellectual discriminative quality (Anubis and Saa), and then performed to your best capacity in a selfless manner.

Sages have given guidelines for which thoughts and actions are in line with the scales of MAAT

The Path of Action and Enlightenment

Adversity in Life

Why is there adversity in life? Wouldn't it be nice if there was no misfortune or unluckiness to hamper your movement in life? Human life abounds with adversity. Even the very rich experience adversity. In fact, no matter who you are you will experience adversity of one form or another as you progress through life.

Adversity is a divine messenger. Imagine how life would be if you could do anything you wanted to do. You would indulge every desire and whim. You would only seek to satisfy your desire for pleasure and you would not accomplish anything significant in life. In the end you would be frustrated and disappointed because no matter how hard you try, it is not possible to ever completely satisfy your desires for the pleasures of the senses.

Adversity is a form of resistance which life places on all beings for the purpose of engendering in them a need to strive to overcome it. When adversity is met with the correct understanding and with the right attitude, it can become a great source of strength and spiritual inspiration. However, if adversity makes you hardhearted, insensitivity, selfish, cold and bitter, then you will lead yourself deeper into the quagmire of negativity and pain. Adversity is God's way of calling your attention away from negative ways of life and to draw attention toward the basic elements of life. Often when people succeed in acquiring some object they desired, they develop conceit and vanity. They look down on others and feel proud of their accomplishment. However, when they lose what they desired, they fall into the valley of adversity, despair, violence and anger. They blame others for their misfortune and seek to hurt others for their loss.

Many of those people who have experienced the most adversity in history include Sages and Saints. Why should God allow those who are trying to be closest to the Divine be plagued with adversity? The answer lies in an ancient Egyptian proverb:

> "Adversity is the seed of well doing; it is the nurse of heroism and boldness; who that hath enough, will endanger himself to have more? Who that is at ease, will set their life on the hazard?
>
> Ancient Egyptian Proverb

Have you noticed that it seems as though the people who are most righteous and deserving of prosperity are the ones who suffer the most in life? In families, the child who is most obedient gets the most attention and disciplinary control. People who are loving and compassionate suffer illnesses and pain from others. This is because nature has been set up by God to create situations which challenge human beings so as to provide for them opportunities to discover their inner resources which give them the capacity to overcome the trouble, and thereby grow in discovery of their deeper Self. Those who suffer most are in reality those who have drawn more attention from the Divine, indeed, chosen for more intense spiritual testing. This testing process of nature allows every soul the opportunity to face trouble with either boldness and faith or with fear and negativity. The rewards of adversity faced well are increased strength of will and an increased feeling of discovery of the Divine within. When adversity is faced with negativity and ignorance, it leads to pain, sorrow and more adversity.

Therefore, adversity cannot be understood and successfully faced with negativity (anger, hatred, hardheartedness, etc.). Adversity can only be overcome with wisdom and virtue, and virtue is the first and most important quality to be developed by all serious spiritual aspirants.

From a spiritual perspective, what is considered to be prosperity by the masses of ignorant people is in reality adversity and what is considered to be adversity by the masses is in reality, prosperity. The masses consider that becoming rich and being able to indulge the pleasures of the senses through food, drink, drugs and sex is the ultimate goal, yet is there anyone who has discovered true peace and contentment because of billions of dollars? Having the opportunity to indulge the pleasures of the senses creates an opportunity for the mind to become more dependent on the worldly pleasures. This process intensifies the egoistic feelings and draws the soul away from discovering true peace within. There is increasing agitation and worry over gaining what is desired and then preoccupation with how to hold onto it. Not realizing that all must be left behind at the time of death, people keep on seeking worldly fame, fortune and glory, and in the process never discover true happiness. They have duped themselves into believing that material wealth brings happiness, because the greedy corporations, the media and popular culture reinforce this message. In reality it is a philosophy of ignorance based on lack of reflection and spiritual insight. Adversity is a call to wake up from this delusion of pain and sorrow and those who are experiencing the worst conditions are receiving the loudest call. Therefore, adversity is in reality prosperity because it stimulates the mind through suffering so that it may look for a higher vision of life and discover the abode of true happiness, peace and contentment which transcends worldly measure.

This exalted vision of life is the innate potential of every human being. What is necessary is the dedication and perseverance to seek a higher understanding of the divine nature of creation and the divine nature of the innermost heart. It has the power to absolve and redeem all negativity. This is the highest goal of all human beings and the most difficult. However, as you gain greater understanding and greater will to act with virtue, your vision of the divine will increase and draw you closer and closer to the Higher Self. This is the glory of virtue and its power to vanquish and eradicate vice from the human heart.

Where Do Sin and Negativity Come From?

When a child is born, does that child know anything about the associations and acquaintances it will make? Does it know about either the good or bad people it will meet? Does it know about the negative things it will do in the future? There are many factors which determine the actions which an individual will perform in their lifetime. The most important of these is the tendency it carried forth from its previous lifetimes. You are not a finite, mortal human being. In reality you are an eternal soul, wandering in the realm of physical nature as you take birth again and again in search of true happiness and peace. Your search has led you to past lives wherein you experienced prosperity and adversity as well as degrees of sinfulness and virtue. If there was a tendency to negative thoughts in the past lifetime, there may be a tendency for more negativity in this lifetime if it is stimulated and not opposed.

The most important thing to remember now is that your present effort can overcome any and all of your past negativity if you apply yourself with earnestness and resolve to become fully established in virtue. This means that you must decide to dedicate your life to discovering and facing all shades of vice and negativity within you and in so doing, never fall back into the pits of ignorance which lead to pain and sorrow.

Having forgotten your eternal nature, you have been wandering through many lifetimes, meeting many other souls in the form of friends, relatives, etc., who are also wandering travelers seeking the same thing as you are: peace and contentment. However, when the soul forgets its eternal nature, it becomes indoctrinated by society and takes on the values and beliefs of society. If society says that money is most important, then the masses of ignorant people do whatever they can to get money. Those who cannot do it legally do it by any other means, because they have lost the connection to their fellow souls due to the delusion of ignorance caused by the pressure of desires and mental agitation. If those around them call them bad, they begin to think "I am a bad person" and then proceed to think of themselves as evil, unconsciously generating thoughts of anger, hatred, envy, etc., which cause them untold miseries though many lifetimes.

In reality, there is no real "badness" in the true you, the deepest part of you. Your Soul is in reality pure, and full of love which is waiting to be discovered. However, your ego is like a blanket of dust which has settled on a piece of glass and obstructs the light from passing through. When you live according to the precepts of virtue, the dust of ignorance, shame, desire, hatred, anger, lust, envy, greed, etc., are removed from your being. Then it is possible for you to discover the treasure which lies within your own heart. Thus, there is in reality no such thing as a criminal heart, only hearts which are clamoring for freedom from the bonds of ignorance and fear.

In reality, there is no real "badness" in the true you

In the ancient Egyptian Myth of Asar, there is a teaching in reference to the god named Set. Set is the embodiment of evil, greed, lust, hatred envy, etc. He killed his own brother (Asar) to steal his Kingdom (Egypt). Heru, Asar' son confronts Set and a battle ensues. Heru eventually overcomes Set through virtue. However, at the end it is revealed that Heru and Set are in reality not two personalities, but indeed one and the same. So the idea behind the teaching is that the true enemy is not outside of you, but within your very own personality, and it exists there in the form of negative qualities which in effect fetter your higher vision of spiritual reality. They cloud your intellect and deteriorate your willpower, so they allow for sinful and unrighteous thoughts to control you and direct your actions. However, the love, sweetness and wisdom of the Divine is also there within you, and this divine essence is equipped with immense spiritual force which can be discovered and used for developing a positive vision which can eradicate all negativity and reveal the true you, as the sun is revealed when the clouds disperse after a storm.

The Path of Action and Enlightenment

Keeping The Balance

"Neither let prosperity put out the eyes of circumspection, nor abundance cut off the hands of frugality; they that too much indulge in the superfluities of life, shall live to lament the want of its necessaries."

"See that prosperity elate not thine heart above measure; neither adversity depress thine mind unto the depths, because fortune beareth hard against you. Their smiles are not stable, therefore build not thy confidence upon them; their frowns endure not forever, therefore let hope teach you patience."

Ancient Egyptian Proverbs

As the proverbs above suggest, equanimity is one of the most important qualities that a spiritual aspirant must develop in order to practice virtuous living. Virtuous living requires strength of will because life is constantly tempting the mind and body toward the pleasures of the senses and toward egoistic desires. When the mind is constantly agitated, swinging back and forth becoming elated and exuberant in prosperous conditions and angry and agitated during adversity the mental energy is drained and dispersed. It becomes hard to concentrate, to act with clarity to distinguish between right and wrong and it becomes more difficult to fulfill the duties of life. This is why in the Egyptian Book of Coming Forth By Day the initiate is constantly saying that he or she *"Kept the Balance"* and is worthy to enter into the divine realms.

Virtuous living requires strength of will

Undue mental agitation is the source of angry thoughts wherein people say and do things they would not otherwise do and get caught up in a pattern wherein they are easily provoked by others who can "push the right buttons" which can anger them. When the mind is in control and always aware of the thoughts within as well as the world outside it is impossible for this mind to fall prey to the provocation of others or to despair or fear. This is the ideal of equanimity that is to be reached by living a virtuous life through the study and practice of the teachings of mystical spirituality.

"No one reaches the beneficent West unless their heart is righteous by doing MAAT. There is no distinction made between the inferior and the superior person; it only matters that one is found faultless when the balances and the two weights stand before the Lord of Eternity. No one is free from the reckoning. Thoth, a baboon, holds the balances to count each one according to what they have done upon earth."

Ancient Egyptian Proverb

Introduction To MAAT PHILOSOPHY

Seek Purity of Heart through an Attitude of Selfless Service:

Always keep in mind that you are performing actions with the grace of God, no matter what actions you perform. God is acting through you to uphold the order of the universe. You are the instrument of the Divine by which the He/She performs actions. Therefore, as you consciously attune yourself to MAAT, you are assisting in the support and positive evolution of the universe. Always keep in mind that as an aspirant, your soul, God, is leading you to certain experiences that are needed for your mental growth. Regardless of your situation, be it an adverse or prosperous situations remember that your goal is to purify your heart so as to come into balance with the cosmic order of the Supreme Being, MAAT. You will realize that many situations which ordinary people, the masses, consider to be adversities, accidents, misfortunes, losses, etc. are in reality opportunities for you to practice your understanding of the teachings and control your ego-personality.

Whatever the situation is that presents itself to you, remember the divine intent behind it and offer your actions in response to it as an oblation or as a presentation made to the Divine as an act of worship. Each time that you remember the Divine throughout the normal course of a day, it is like taking a trip to a temple or holy site. When you offer your actions to the Divine and accept no egoistic credit for the actions, it is an even higher form of worship of the Divine. When you inwardly take the attitude that it is in reality the Divine Self who is acting and not you, this is the highest form of worship of the Divine. If you were able to maintain this form of awareness continuously you would achieve spiritual realization in a short time.

All things are in reality a manifestation of the Divine. Just as a candle's light and heat are one and the same, the manifestation (universe) and the Divine Self are one and the same. Therefore, the idea that there are individuals acting independently as various people with different names is an illusion backed up by mental ignorance. You must continue to assert this truth at all times in order to combat that ignorance and thereby purify your heart.

> All things are in reality a manifestation of the Divine.

Seek Purity of Heart by Not Expecting a Reward For Your Actions

In performing your actions, never seek an external reward. Always feel that you are performing actions for the Divine Self in an effort to purify your heart of egoistic feelings and sentiments. External expectations and rewards for your actions are always bound to be fleeting and cannot be counted on. Therefore, if you base your happiness on something that is fleeting, you are basing it on an illusion which will certainly lead to disappointment and unrest. Remember the definition of reality: that which is unchanging. Seek deep within you for what is unchanging regardless of the external situations. Seek for the eternal witnessing Self within you who is separate from the thoughts and transitory situations of the external world. Perform your actions well but do not become attached to them as sources of your happiness.

"They who revere MAAT are long lived;
they who are covetous have no tomb."

-Ancient Egyptian Proverb

The Path of Action and Enlightenment

In reality, it is the soul within you that gives meaning and worth to all externalities. Therefore, your soul is the source of all understanding, meaning and awareness. This soul is full of immense happiness (bliss) and you can discover this inward peace and happiness by inwardly discovering your true Self and not seeking happiness from objects outside of yourself. Seeking happiness and the fulfillment of desires through worldly pursuits and relationships only lead to frustrations and more desires. This constant fanning of the waves of the mind with the thoughts of desires and cravings survives in the innermost recesses of the unconscious mind, embedded deep within the astral and causal bodies of the human being. These deep karmic impressions in the unconscious mind, which remain after the death of the physical body, lead the soul to astral heavens and hells, and to future embodiments in physical form.

Seek Purity of Heart Through Your Work Occupation and Daily Activities:

> *"Do not disturb a great person or distract their attention when they are occupied, trying to understand their task. When they are thus occupied they strip their body through love of what they do. Love for the work which they do brings people closer to God.*
> *These are the people who succeed in what they do."*
>
> Ancient Egyptian Proverb

Another profound insight into the teachings of MAAT is that you should always strive to perform work that is in harmony with your nature. As an expression of the Divine Self, you are endowed with unlimited capabilities and you should not allow your fears or the desires of others to limit the unfoldment of those energies. You must strive to allow yourself to gradually develop a sense of what is right for you. This occurs when you begin to develop peace and harmony within yourself. You will discover which jobs to pursue on the basis of your inner desire, rather than the superficial desire of your ego-self which wants to pursue a job or occupation because it looks glamorous or lucrative.

Ancient Egyptian civilization placed high importance on the occupation of the individual

Ancient Egyptian civilization placed high importance on the occupation of the individual due to these very reasons. Many people suffer through life because they have made the wrong choices about their chosen profession or occupation and feel stuck and unable to change their lot in life. Sometimes they are led by their families, or their own greed or fear, into pursuing occupations for the wrong reasons. You must understand that if you choose an occupation or career just to make money or because you have been told that some particular profession is in demand, etc., you may make some money at it but you will end up being miserable and disappointed with the work you have chosen as well as your life in general. Your career will truly become "work." It will not be fulfilling because you are not doing it out of the goodness of your heart. Eventually, it will become a struggle and a burden. Also, you will not develop divine qualities and mental peace which will lead you toward Enlightenment, such as patience, contentment, forgiveness universal love, compassion, etc. Rather, your ego (ignorant and disturbed state of mind) will become more hardened and you will use unrighteous means to make money so that you can make money. You may sell things to people even though you know they do not need them or deal in products which you know are harmful. All the while, your intellect, which is dulled by the desires, cravings and longings of the lower mind and senses for egoistic pleasures, will justify the unrighteous actions. However, the impressions of longing and desire as well as the contradictions of your own conscience become registered in the deep unconscious and create a basis for heaven or hell on earth as well as beyond. This is a profound teaching which you need to reflect upon seriously.

Even though people who live and acquire wealth in this "Setian" manner seem happy with the wealth, in reality there is unrest in their "hearts" (minds). In fact, most people have been convinced that wealth is or brings happiness and this is the view of ignorance promoted by society at large and the media. While there is nothing wrong with having spiritual and material wealth, most people who are ignorant of spiritual truths become dependent and attached to their wealth as a source of pleasure and happiness and are therefore, bound to pursue, hoard and protect their wealth in order to be happy. However, this happiness which requires continued mental agitation and worry is no happiness at all. Even if you develop a prosperous situation for yourself, your worries and anxieties will not protect you from addictions, cravings and other forms of pain which the world abounds with. Therefore, happiness, and consequently true wealth, is not to be found in objects or possessions of the world. It is a state of mind which can be discovered through spiritual insight. The impressions lodged in the unconscious mind form a storehouse of restless desires which will lead to repeated embodiments and deprive you from discovering the peace of your Self.

There is nothing wrong with having spiritual and material wealth

Thus, while there seems to be little justice in the world, no deed goes unseen by MAAT who is the Self, the all-seeing Soul who supports all human activity and the cosmos. This Self is your very own innermost essence, therefore, you are essentially MAAT. You are the judge and jury of your own actions. Since you are ultimately the controller of your own actions as well as the judge of them, you can change your entire being by learning the ways of MAAT and eradicating the negativity and ignorance you have built up in this lifetime as well as the previous ones. This can be accomplished by following the teachings outlined in the scriptures. Before blindly moving into worldly actions examine yourself first.

Ask yourself: *Do I need this relationship or this object or is it just to satisfy my ego's desire for lust, pleasure or greed? Is this action I am about to do going to help me simplify my life or will it complicate it more? Will it bring peace of mind or will it cause more agitation?* If it is for the ego it is a waste of time because the ego cannot be satisfied since it is an endless pit of desire!

This process of introspection and self-awareness begins to break the cycle of actions performed out of weak will and ignorance which lead to pain and sorrow later on.

The Path of Action and Enlightenment

Choosing an occupation:

Many people are afraid to choose some occupation which is what they would really like to be doing because they fear where their next meal will come from, how they will be supported, etc. But didn't Jesus say:

> Matthew 6:*28 And why are ye anxious for raiment? Consider the lilies of the field, how they grow; they toil not, neither do they spin:*
> *29 And yet I say to you, That even Solomon in all his glory was not arrayed like one of these.*
> *30 Wherefore, if God so clotheth the grass of the field, which to day is, and to morrow is cast into the oven, [shall he] not much more [clothe] you, O ye of little faith?*

This teaching exists in all major world philosophies. The task of the aspirant is to go beyond the fears of human existence. This is done by adopting the study of spiritual teachings and reflecting upon then with the assistance of the spiritual preceptor. Gradually, you will discover an occupation that resonates with your internal feeling. You will find something that you would do even if you were not paid. When this happens you will not be motivated by selfish motives and the work itself will be rewarding to you and to society. You will begin to discover a form of peace which is not achieved by most people. This will assist you to have a peaceful disposition which will allow you to progress further in your spiritual discipline. So don't worry, you are a child of the universe and when you tread the path of spiritual aspiration, even though it may be difficult at some times, you will be provided for. This is a spiritual law. The key is continued effort in your spiritual disciplines. Strive to understand the teachings no matter how many times you fail. Gradually incorporate meditation, recitations of words of power, study of the scriptures and remembrance of the divine throughout the day and you will be led to works which are in harmony with your nature.

The key is continued effort in your spiritual disciplines.

Seek Purity of Heart Through Living a Life of Simplicity

> "When opulence and extravagance are a necessity instead of righteousness and truth, society will be governed by greed and injustice."
>
> Ancient Egyptian Proverb

The key to reducing worldly entanglements and negative karmic impressions which will lead to future pain and reincarnation is to reduce the desires in the mind. One important way to accomplish this is to simplify one's life. This implies reducing one's karmic entanglements and worries which constantly agitate the mind. We are indoctrinated into believing that material wealth brings happiness, so much so that having achieved a measure of success, according to societal standards, we convince ourselves that we are happy, sometimes even if it means an early grave due to overwork and increased stress attempting to support luxuries which are not needed or pursuing ideals which are wrong for us. Many who may not have the material wealth are as if hypnotized by the idea that they "must" pursue it and once achieved, it will yield the long sought after happiness. Despite the disappointments and frustrations, we continue to pursue the dream, not realizing that material wealth does not automatically produce happiness. Further, if those who have achieved the riches are happy, it is not because of the riches but due to a much deeper psychological integration that has occurred. Also, just as the presence of material wealth does not necessarily constitute prosperity, mental peace and happiness, in the same way, the lack of material wealth does not necessarily constitute adversity, mental agitation or unhappiness.

A life of simplicity does not mean giving up all wealth and going to live off the land. It means living according to the necessities of life and not hoarding possessions as sources of happiness or due to some family obligation. It means not indulging in the egoism of jealousy by comparing oneself to others and trying to emulate their success or trying to look good in their eyes. The divine plan has prescribed a specific path for every individual. Therefore, you should live life according to the understanding that you have been given all of the necessary tools to accomplish the goals of your life. Therefore, while continuing to strive for better conditions in life the underlying understanding should be that if riches are to come it is by the will of the Divine. Likewise, if adversities come it is for the same reason. Both adversities and prosperities come to a person according to their karmic history as fruits of past actions. Therefore, in order to promote positive situations in the future, all you need to do is concentrate on correct actions in the present which are guided by the correct attitude and understanding.

Simplicity means living within one's means and watching over the mind's desires for pleasures and luxuries that are not necessary, accepting whatever comes as part of the divine plan, even while striving to better oneself. In this way, feelings of detachment, contentment and peace can be developed even while you are engaged in actions which are necessary in life.

Simplicity means living within one's means and watching over the mind's desires

The Philosophy of Action in the Egyptian Book of Coming Forth By Day

> *"No one reaches the beneficent West unless their heart is righteous by doing MAAT. There is no distinction made between the inferior and the superior person; it only matters that one is found faultless when the balances and the two weights stand before the Lord of Eternity. No one is free from the reckoning. Thoth, a baboon, holds the balances to count each one according to what they have done upon earth."*
>
> Ancient Egyptian Proverb

The principal issue of the *Egyptian Book of Coming Forth By Day* is whether or not the initiate has been able to purify his/her heart and thereby pass the test of the scales. This judgment does not only occur at the time of death but it occurs at every moment of your life. You are always being tested in your resolve and your wisdom through day to day situations that arise. The objective is to be clear of wrongdoing (actions which take you away from self-realization) and to realize your identity with the Divine through selfless actions. You should not have preferences of one object over another or one person over another because all things in creation are equally endowed with divine essence, and you are one with that essence. Therefore, what is there to desire? What is there to prefer? You are all and all is you. Therefore, remain in a peaceful state at all times and through all conditions, remaining steadfast in your true Self.

This is the true meaning of the identification of the initiate with the Supreme Being. In the Asarian Mysteries, the initiate's name is changed to Asar. This signifies that the initiate needs to identify himself/herself not with the transient personality but with the part which is eternal and all-encompassing. Therefore, your true name is Asar. The true name of everyone you know is also Asar and the essence of all the different objects of creation (the Neters which have assumed different forms and qualities) is also Asar. Now with this understanding, close your eyes and reflect on this supreme truth before proceeding with the following section. Reflect on the findings of modern physics, how all things have an infinite origin. Now go beyond your body consciousness and the thoughts of yourself as a body and begin to see yourself as infinite, immortal and eternal.

The Concept of The "Doer" and the "Non-doer" in Maat Philosophy

A meditative lifestyle should be developed along with one's formal meditation practices. This means acting in such a way that there is greater and greater detachment from objects and situations and greater independence and peace within. This can only occur when there is a keen understanding of one's deeper self and the nature of the world of human experience along with formal meditation practices and other activities which promote physical health (diet and exercise). Ordinarily, people "do" things in order to gain some objective or to derive some pleasure or reward. From a yogic or Buddhist perspective they are "doers of action." They act out of the unconscious and subconscious desires arising in the mind at any given time and are thus, beset with a perpetual state of unrest and agitation. The meditative way of life means that your actions are always affirmations of your higher knowledge and awareness and not based on the unconscious desires and emotions of the mind. The perfection in this discipline only comes with practice. When this art is perfected the practitioner is referred to as a "non-doer." This is because even though they may be doing many things in their life, in reality they have discovered that the true rewards of life do not depend on the outcome of an activity, its fruit or reward.

The main difference between a doer and a non-doer

The main difference between a doer and a non-doer is that the doer is driven by desires while the non-doer is indifferent to the desires of the mind and the fruits of the action they are performing. The non-doer acts out of wakefulness while the doer acts out of a desire filled mind. Thus, the non-doer can never be disappointed or made unhappy because of a situation in life while the doer is always engaged in a roller coaster of elation or depression, happiness or sorrow, pain or pleasure, etc., never finding an abiding peace   The non-doer acts out of necessity and is primarily concerned with experiencing the moment fully while carrying out the present task to perfection, not worrying about the rewards for the task. Thus, it may be said that for the non-doer there is an immediate reward of peace and joy whereas the doer is always looking to the future or the past. Their peace and happiness does not come from expectations of the future nor do they experience sorrow due to some negative situation which occurred in the past. They have discovered a deep experience in the present which transcends both past and future. Thus, they experience a unique form of peace and happiness in an eternal present which is not affected by the various ups and downs of life. Adversity and prosperity are an integral part of human existence. The belief that life can or should only be composed of happy or positive situations is a factor of philosophical ignorance and a lack of reflection on history. A wise person realizes that life is full of adverse as well as prosperous situation. While trying to promote the prosperous situations there must be expectation of adversity as well. This wisdom leads to the understanding that the world and worldly situations cannot be relied upon as a source of happiness. There will always arise some situation which will bring any form of worldly prosperity to an end. Therefore, a wise person does not become attached to worldly objects, people or situations even while being involved with them in various situations during the normal course of a lifetime.

General society believes that actions are to be performed for the goal of attaining some objective which will yield a reward. The socialization process teaches the individual to seek to perform actions because this is the way to attain something which will cause happiness. This is the predicament of the masses of people who have not studied Yoga or Mystical Philosophies such as Buddhism, Shetaut Neter or Vedanta. The following line from the Declaration of Independence illustrates this point succinctly.

> We hold these truths to be self-evident, that all men are created equal, that they are endowed by their Creator with certain unalienable Rights, that among these are Life, Liberty and the **pursuit of happiness**.

There is nothing wrong with pursuing happiness. In fact, this is the innermost drive of the human heart. The problem comes when this pursuit is engaged in with a sense of ignorance and delusion which most people display. Most people do not know what true happiness is so they pursue wealth, progeny, fame and the pleasures of the senses. Along with this there is greater effectiveness and perfection in one's actions.

There is nothing wrong with pursuing happiness.

The Path of Action and Enlightenment

Actions of any type will always lead to some result. However, this result is not as predictable as people have come to believe. In reality, the only thing a human being can control is the action itself and not the fruits of the action. If there is concentration on the action without desire or expectation of the fruits of the action, then there can be peace and contentment even while the action is being performed. This is the way of the non-doer. Actions performed with expectations and desire are the way of the doer. The non-doer is free from the fruits because he/she is free from desires and expectations while the doer is dependent on the actions and is bound to the results be they positive or negative. When desires and expectation in the mind are resolved the mind becomes calm and peaceful. Under these conditions the non-doer is free from elation or depression because His/her pleasure is coming from the present action in the present moment and is not based on memories of the past of pleasurable situations which are impelling a movement to repeat those activities or on expectations for the future activities which will somehow bring happiness. The non-doer, not being bound

When desires and expectation in the mind are resolved the mind becomes calm to the memories or to the expectations is not bound by either the past nor the future and thereby discovers an eternal present. The doer is always caught up in the past or the present and thereby loses the opportunity to discover peace and true happiness. This is the condition of most people in the world. Before they realize it their entire life has gone by without their being aware of the passage of time. This is the art of true spiritual life. It leads one to detach from the world even while continuing to live in it and thereby to discover the hidden inner spiritual dimensions of the unconscious mind and what lies beyond. The doer is always bound to a form of experience which is determined by and bound to the world of time and space because only in time and space can there manifest the memories of the past and the expectations for the future. The non-doer eventually discovers a transcendental experience of expanding consciousness in the present moment.

The philosophy of meditation in action (reflecting on one's actions) may seem foreign to you at first but if you reflect upon it you will discover that it holds great truth as well as great potential to assist you in discovering abiding peace and harmony in your life. When you begin to practice and discover how wonderful it is to be in control of your mind instead of being prey to the positive or negative emotions and desires you will discover an incomparable feeling which goes beyond the ordinary concept of happiness. As with other human endeavors, in order to gain success you need to study the philosophy intensively with great concentration and then practice it in your day to day life. Treat it as an experiment. The world and your life will not go away. Just ask yourself: What would happen if I was to become less attached and more in control of my mind? Follow the teachings and discover the inner resources you need to discover true happiness and to overcome the obstacles of life.

The Self which is the innermost essence of every human being, "saves" the individual when they turn to the Self as the only reality. This turning toward the Self, instead of indulging in the egoism of the mind, destroys the possibility of any danger in the realm of time and space or in the astral planes. This is what Jesus referred to when he spoke about guarding against robbers. The robbers are the evils of egoism and ignorance (anger, hate, lust, etc.). For one who is watchful, there can be no surprise. For one who is not aware, there is always surprise and unexpected tragedy. By giving importance and primacy to these thieves instead of to the Self, these thieves become the reality of the mind and through identification with the mind, the soul is drawn to experience the fate of karmic entanglements of time and space existence. For they who turn to the Self, even if there were mountainous negative karmic impressions in the mind (heart), self-effort will mitigate those karmas in the same way that soap cleanses impurity. You are the creator of your destiny. Since God is your intrinsic reality, there is no one to look to for redemption other than yourself. You caused your own existence in this time and place and it is you who are responsible for the conditions of your incarnation and the situations in life which you find yourself. Also, since your innermost reality beyond the ego is the Divine Self, you have infinite resources to achieve any goal, transform yourself, and change your entire life. Therefore, through the science of yoga, you can develop the understanding of the mind which will enable you to effect miraculous changes within yourself. This is the magic of wisdom.

Since your innermost reality beyond the ego is the Divine Self, you have infinite resources

The Path of Action and Enlightenment

MAAT and The Serpent Power

Maat Philosophy is intimately related to the teaching of the Arat Shekhem (Serpent Power). The Arat Shekhem is a dormant life force which every human being possesses. It activates in accordance with a person's level of virtue. That is, the more virtuous the person, the more the life force awakens and as it awakens it leads a human being to the heights of spiritual enlightenment. This process happens automatically so it is important to lead a life of virtue which leads to *Maat ab* or purity of heart. The following images come from papyruses known as *Prt m Hru* or Book of Enlightenment. For more details on the Serpent Power see the books *The Serpent Power* and *The Book of the Dead* by Muata Ashby.

The ancient Egyptian *Greenfield Papyrus* and the Egyptian *Book of Coming Forth By Day of Kenna*, which are both treatises of the Asarian Resurrection religion of ancient Egypt contain important teachings in reference to what was in ancient times called *"Arat Sekhem"* or "Serpent Power," and is today commonly known as Kundalini Yoga in India. We explored both of these in the book *Egyptian Yoga: The Philosophy of Enlightenment* and here we will discuss some more advanced theory related to the Serpent Power and the first level of Serpent Power Yoga meditation. There is an audio tape meditation series which follows along with this section. If you are interested in the audio workshop and meditation music contact the publisher, or book distributor.

The subject of life force energy and the sublimation of sexual energy into spiritual energy existed many thousands of years in Egypt prior to its development in modern India under the name *Kundalini Yoga*. It later appears in many parts of the world but it did not find extensive documentation until the Sages of India composed the voluminous scriptures in relation to Kundalini Yoga.

The Egyptian Seven Powers are related to the seven energy centers of the subtle body.

As in the Indian Chakra System, the Egyptian Seven Powers are related to the seven energy centers of the subtle body which are not visible to the ordinary eye and are in the same space as the physical spine though not in the same plane as the physical body. They are linked to the awakening of one's spiritual powers and consciousness. As one progresses on their spiritual path of evolution, while either purposely employing a yogic spiritual discipline (study and application of spiritual and philosophic scriptures, reflection and meditation) or learning through the process of trial and error, these centers will automatically open, allowing one to experience increasing communion with the higher self: GOD. The process of raising one's spiritual power may be aided by specific exercises such as concentration, proper breathing, meditation on the meanings of the spiritual symbols and surrendering to the will of the Higher Self (GOD). These techniques allow one to transform one's waking personality so that one may discover their innermost self: GOD. This should be done under the guidance of a qualified teacher (spiritual master).

The energy centers of the subtle body are likened to a tree which the aspirant climbs through personality integration, which leads to intuitional realization of the transcendental self. In the process of creation, the creative energy manifests in the form of six planes of consciousness. This is the realm of phenomenal reality including physical, astral and mental existence. Most people exist on the level of the first three energy-consciousness levels. The goal of this Yoga is to unite the six phenomenal consciousness centers with the seventh or transcendental realm of consciousness, the

Introduction To MAAT PHILOSOPHY

Absolute. This absolute is what various religions refer to by different names such as the Kingdom of Heaven, Asar, Krishna, Brahman, the Tao, etc.

Kundalini energy flows throughout thousands of *Nadis* or energy channels which is known as Prana, chi, Ra-Sekhem. If any of the energy channels are blocked or over-sensitized, a dis-balance can arise, causing illness in the mind and physical body. There are three most important channels through which Kundalini flows. These are: the *Sushumna, Ida and Pingala* -These are represented by the Egyptian Caduceus of Djehuti which is composed of a staff which has two serpents wrapped around it.

The state of enlightenment is further described in chapter 83 and 85 where the initiate realizes that the seven Uraeus deities or bodies (immortal parts of the spirit) have been reconstituted:

> ***"The seven Uraeuses are my body...***
> ***my image is now eternal."***

These seven Uraeuses are also described as the *"seven souls of Ra"* and *"the seven arms of the balance (Maat)."*

How does the practice of virtue affect the Life Force energy in an individual? When an individual lives life based on ignorance, in an imbalanced way, energy is dissipated and the mind is agitated. The Life Force energy that could have been used to control the mind and direct it to concentrate on discovering divine qualities and peace, has been lost. Such an individual will live a life of anxiety and restlessness as previously described.

If the energy that would have been used chasing after possessions, sensual pleasures, and mental agitation were to be conserved, this very energy would allow the individual to discover increasing peace and happiness from within, culminating in discovery of the innermost spiritual Self, the Higher Self. The picture from the Papyrus of Kenna shows Ammit, the monster who devours the unrighteous. Notice that she is biting the scales of MAAT between the third and fourth circles. These circles indicate levels of spiritual evolution or psycho-spiritual energy centers. The Greenfield Papyrus shows the centers as a chain with seven links. These centers refer to the judgment of the heart of the initiate. Centers 1-3 indicate immature human beings who live to seek sensual pleasures and centers 4-7 indicate individuals who are progressing on the spiritual path.

Notice that she is biting the scales of MAAT between the third and fourth circles.

The Path of Action and Enlightenment

Below- Left-The Ancient Egyptian Papyrus Greenfield (British Museum) displaying the rings signifying the serpentine path of the Life Force, and the levels of spiritual consciousness or *Arat Shekhem* (Serpent Power) and the *Sefech Ba Ra* (7 Life Force energy centers or Psycho-spiritual consciousness centers)

Below: Papyrus Qenna (Leyden Museum), displaying the spheres signifying the serpentine path of the Life Force from the Spirit above to the heart below, and the levels of spiritual consciousness, the *Sefech Ba Ra* (7 Life Force energy centers or Psycho-spiritual consciousness centers)

Above: Ancient Egyptian artistic representation of the yogi seated in the lotus posture displaying the three main channels of the *Arat Shekhem* (Serpent Power) and the *Sefech Ba Ra* (7 Life Force energy centers) 5th dynasty (4th millennium B.C.E.)

The energy centers (chakras) wherein the Life Force energy is transformed from subtle to gross energy for use by the body are seven in number and are depicted as follows.

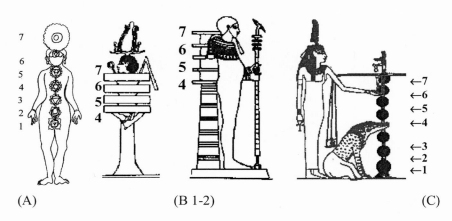

(A) (B 1-2) (C)

Left (A), the East Indian rendition of the Life Force energy centers (chakras) in the subtle spine of the individual.

Center (B 1-2), Ptah-Asar-Ancient Egyptian rendition of the Life Force energy centers in the subtle spine of the individual. The god Asar displays the four upper centers as centers of higher consciousness.

The figure at right (C) shows the scale of Maat displaying the seven spheres or energy centers called the *"seven souls of Ra"* and *"the seven arms of the balance (Maat)."*

Figure (C), above, includes the Ammit demon, (composite beast combining one third hippopotamus, one third lion and one third crocodile), symbolic devourer of unrighteous souls, biting between the 3rd & 4th sphere (energy center-chakra). This means that those who have not attained a consciousness level higher than the 3rd

center will continue to suffer and reincarnate. The spheres represent levels of spiritual consciousness from the most ignorant (1) to the most enlightened (7). The lower three spheres are related to worldly consciousness and the upper four are related to spiritual consciousness and enlightenment, therefore, the lower must be sublimated into the higher levels. This is the project of spiritual evolution. Those who have attained the higher (3rd through the 7th) centers will move on and attain enlightenment. This Kamitan system of energy spheres and the Caduceus with its central shaft symbolizing the subtle spine, and the two intertwining serpents, symbolizing the dual energies into which the central shaft differentiates, concurs in every detail with the later developments in East Indian Mysticism encompassed by the discipline known as Kundalini Yoga with its system of Chakras and the three main energy channels, Sushumna (central) and Ida and Pingala (intertwining conduits).

Those who have attained the higher (3rd through the 7th) centers will move on and attain enlightenment.

Left-An East Indian depiction of the Chakras with the Sushumna (central) and Ida and Pingala (intertwining conduits).

Two Center images- left - the Hermetic[19] Caduceus with the central Shaft (Asar), and the intertwining serpents (Uadjit and Nekhebit, also known as Aset and Nebethet); right-Ancient caduceus motif: Asar with the serpent goddesses.

Far Right- The Kamitan Energy Consciousness Centers (depicted as Spheres-Chakras or serpentine chains)

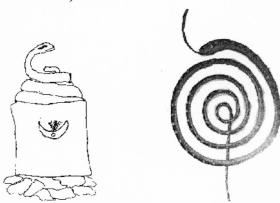

Above left: the Arat Serpent of Ancient Egyptian mysticism (Basket of Isis) showing the classic 3 ½ turns of the Serpent Power. Above right: the Kundalini Serpent of Indian mysticism showing the classic 3 ½ turns of the Serpent Power.

---

[19] Late Ancient Egyptian motif.

Introduction To MAAT PHILOSOPHY

The Illumination of The Mind With The Truth of Maat.

The human mind perceives everything according to the pairs of opposites and therefore sees itself as a subject in a world of other subjects and objects. When the mind is transcended, the duality of the mind which leads to the triad of perception is also transcended. Think about it. You cannot think of differences, here-there, up-down, etc. if you go beyond your thoughts. Even if you are not an adept meditator who can stop the thoughts of the mind for long periods, you should be able to concentrate the mind for a few seconds. The awareness of the world ceases during that time. This is basically what happens whenever you really concentrate on something. Reflect on those moments where you were trying to remember something intensely. What was your experience in that moment? In this moment there are no thoughts or awareness of the world. This is similar to what occurs in the dreamless sleep state. The difference is that when in the dreamless sleep state you are not aware of it.

When this transcendental experience occurs, there is once again the experience of the oneness of existence. The illusion of the mind has dissolved back into the primordial ocean of infinite being from which the creation arose. This is the conscious perception of a liberated sage endowed with enlightenment. The enlightened sage perceives him/herself as that primordial God who arose out of the primeval waters with the original thought and the entire creations is that same primeval ocean which only appeared to change into the multiplicity of the various objects of creation but never did truly did undergo an irreversible *transformation*. In this manner, the discipline of Maat, or the practice of living according to what is real and true, leads to the conscious perception of that which is real and true.

The oneness which is discovered within the vast darkness of the mind is the objective of all spiritual disciplines. If you were to remain within this darkness long enough and were able to penetrate it deeply enough you would discover that it is not void or empty. This void is in reality pure potential being or the primeval ocean of undifferentiated consciousness which lies in the deeper levels of the mind. The illusion of the mind which causes ordinary human consciousness to arise has dissolved back into the primordial ocean of infinite being from which it arose as a wave rises out of and recedes back into the ocean. Creation implies your perception of the world as a world rather than as Neter. A liberated Sage sees the world as it truly is, a manifestation of Neter through the Neters. While the Neters appear as objects in a world of time and space to the ignorant masses, the Sage knows them to be expressions of the Divine in much the same way as everything in your dream is in reality an expression of your mind.

A liberated Sage sees the world

Furthermore, a Liberated Sage perceives him/herself as the primordial ocean from which all arises through thoughts. Thus, what is considered to be existence is in reality a set of thoughts from the cosmic mind which have stirred up in the ocean of primeval consciousness. Consciousness is devoid of time and space. It is eternal and ever abiding. Therefore, the universe and the primeval ocean are understood to be one and the same by an enlightened Sage while unenlightened people see a world full of a multiplicity of objects which exist in time and space. Most people are unaware of this level of consciousness and remain as if at the surface of an ocean experiencing themselves, other living beings and objects in the world as various waves rising and continually falling, sometimes rising and receding gently and at other times crashing into each other with great force. When you are on the surface of the ocean you may experience gentle conditions or you may experience being buffeted. However, if you go down deep enough you will experience absolute tranquility even if there is a raging storm up above. This diving deep into the ocean of consciousness is accomplished through the various practices of yoga: studying the teachings, meditation, selfless service, promoting Hetep in all situations, etc.

In this manner, the discipline of Maat, or the practice of living according to what is real and true, leads to the conscious realization or perception of that which is real and true. At the deepest level the source of all things is to be discovered. This source is variously known as Asar, Amun, Nebertcher, Aset etc., and this source is also your innermost Self.

The body is of the earth, the soul belongs to heaven
Ancient Egyptian Proverb

As stated earlier, Maat is that which is *true* and that which is true is *ceaseless and regular* from beginning to end. Therefore, all developments in between the beginning and the end which seem to arise and fall, to be born, to have life and to die, are in reality illusions of the mind. A keen insight into the wisdom of the four states of consciousness (waking, dream, dreamless-sleep) and into the teachings of Maat provide an effective means to traverse the miseries of human existence and to lead the aspirant to the innermost shrine, the abode of absolute truth which is symbolized by the aspirants movements closer and closer to the holy of holies where Asar is located. The aspirant moves closer and closer to Asar as he/she passes the tests of the various assessors of Maat or the 42 gods and goddesses who uphold each of the 42 major precepts of Maat. This, coupled with the identification of the name of the aspirant with that of Asar symbolizes the attunement of the initiate with his/her innermost cosmic being which is identical with that of the Supreme Being (Asar). The belief in the physical body and of the human personality as being real and abiding is *untruth*, while the belief in the human soul as the abiding, eternal "real" self is the truth. The soul, which is the innermost reality of your essence and the sustainer of your astral and physical bodies, is the true essence of your being. The discipline of Maat is the way or vehicle to achieve this realization in conscious fact.

It must be clearly understood that the practice of Maat or righteous action alone without the wisdom of the Self will not lead to supreme perfection. Initiatic (yogic) wisdom and the humility which develop with selfless service are necessary to promote understanding of the truth in much the same way that dirt is cleansed with soap. There are many who follow the teachings of righteousness and may even be sincere, however, they do not achieve higher spiritual realization nor are they able to control the egoism of the mind. At times they may seem humble, forthright and at peace and at other times they may have flights of passion, anger, and may be tormented with the continued flow of desires (mental and physical). The mental state of conflict persists because they have not proceeded beyond the intellectual level of

There are many who follow the teachings of righteousness and may even be sincere, however, they do not achieve higher spiritual realization

111

the teaching. They have not been able to achieve higher spiritual realization of the inner truths which lie beyond the conscious mind.

If you use your mind and senses in order to determine what is real, what is a cause of happiness and what is not, etc. you are using an incomplete method which will always fall short. Your soul longs for the entire truth of its true nature. The mind and senses can only perceive minuscule pieces of that truth. The mind is limited and therefore, cannot perceive the truth in its totality. Therefore, there is always some lingering unfulfilled desire. Absolute Truth and transcendental peace which leads to mastery over the relative world cannot be found by intellectually perfecting one's knowledge of the wisdom teachings. So whenever the mind is used you will encounter imperfect perceptions which are limited by the notions of the mind and the ability of the senses. The only way to perceive the truth is to not used the mind and senses.

This idea may be likened to a group of blind people who are touching a pyramid. Each one uses their available senses of touch. One may think it is a slanted wall, another may think it is a mountain, another may think it is a house. All of these analyses are preposterous for someone who has the faculty of sight. All at once the complete structure is taken in by the faculty of sight. All at once the image is perceived in its entirety. This is the way in which transcendental intuition works as opposed to the mind and senses. The mind and senses constrict your inner vision because your are holding on to them due to your ignorant understanding of your true nature. Your clinging to your ego concept forces you to use the mind and senses because only with the mind and senses is it possible to perceive yourself as a separate ego personality. You must transcend the fear of giving up the ego and dive deeply into the transcendental realms of consciousness. When you are able to do this you will discover the deeper levels of consciousness which you possess and you will view the ego and waking state as transitory extensions of your true self.

There must be a deep transformation which reaches down to the innermost reaches of your heart (subconscious and unconscious levels of mind). Otherwise you will continue to be caught in the realm of conflict (battle of Heru and Set), and will not be able to attain mastery over the mind. This is the predicament of the lower mental states of consciousness and it is symbolizes in the disintegration of the body of Asar. The mind is chopped into many pieces. In reality it is the delusion of the mind, its ignorance, which causes it to believe in the triad effect. When the triad is transcended through the practices of yoga, the mind (heart) is cleared of all impurities and is then worthy to behold that which is the only reality.

This is the predicament of the lower mental states of consciousness

There is one most important factor in the spiritual discipline which must be accomplished in order to be victorious over the lower nature. This factor is the effacement of the ego. In order to approach God you must act and think as God (according to the precepts of Maat) while losing your identification with your self as an individual personality and affirming your innermost divine essence which is one with the Supreme divine essence. These teachings are to be practiced at all times and under all conditions.

The Path of Action and Enlightenment

The practice of virtuous living must include the effacement of the ego it it is to reach its height. You cannot become perfectly free of desires, vices, ulterior motives, jealousy, greed and so forth if you internally harbor egoism within you, the idea "I am an individual." The perfection of virtue means that you have a keen understanding that you are not the body, mind, senses, desires or cravings, etc. You are beyond these. It is this idea which allows you to rise above pettiness, greed and egoistic desires and it also allows you to restrain yourself and to refrain from engaging in activities which you know will bring only disappointment and frustration in the long run.

The Mystical Meaning of The Voyage of Ra

The ancient Egyptian Creation Myth tells of the emergence of Ra, out of the primeval ocean. The ocean was unformed, undifferentiated matter. The emergence of Ra was synonymous with the coagulation of matter into various forms. In so doing, Ra established MAAT (order) in the place of Chaos.

The voyage of Ra is depicted as two boats. One travels through Nut (the heavens) during the day while shining upon the Geb (physical world). The other travels through the Duat (Netherworld) at night and provides the light of consciousness which shines in the astral world.

The Barque of Ra-Tem *Mandjet*  (i.e. the movement of the Self) courses through all regions of existence including the earth (physical plane or realm) and the *Sekhet-hetepet* or *Duat* (astral plane or realm). Ra possessed another barque known as the *Mesektet,* the boat which travels in the nighttime through the Duat or Amentet (astral-intermediate plane) of disembodied souls and the transcendental world which is the peaceful abode of those who join with Ra (God).

Truth of Speech

The mouth

The symbol of the mouth is of paramount importance in Ancient Egyptian Mystical wisdom and particularly in the philosophy of MAAT. The mouth is a symbol of consciousness and it is the mouth which is used in two of the most important mystical teachings of ancient Egyptian Yoga, The Creation and the Opening of the Mouth Ceremony of the Book of Coming Forth By Day.

thoughts are conditioning instruments.

Consider the following. When you think of anything you attach words to your thoughts. In fact, it is difficult to think without words. Therefore, words are the symbols which the human mind uses to group thoughts and which constitute intellectual forms of understanding. However, thoughts are conditioning instruments. This means that when you think you are actually differentiating. The differentiating process allows the mind to be conscious or aware of differences in matter so it labels these differences with different names based on the form or function of the object or the relationship it has to it.

The mind learns to call objects by names. For example a chair is an aggregate of matter just like a rock. However, the mind has learned to call it a particular name and to associate the name "chair" with a particular king of object which looks in a particular way and which serves a particular function.

When the mind goes beyond words it is going beyond thoughts and thereby experiences undifferentiated consciousness. This is the deeper implication of the opening of the mouth ceremony. It signifies opening the consciousness and memory of the undifferentiated state because although at a lower state of spiritual evolution consciousness appears to be differentiated, the underlying essence is undifferentiated. When intuitional realization or spiritual enlightenment dawns in the human mind, words are no longer viewed as differentiating instruments, but merely as practical instruments for the spirit to operate and interact with the world through a human personality. This is the difference between a human being who is spiritually enlightened and one who is caught in the state of ignorance and egoism.

The vocal capacity in a human being is intimately related to the unconscious level of the mind. This is why those who do not practice introspection and self control often blurt out thing they do not wish to say and which they regret later. For this reason, the teachings enjoin that a spiritual aspirant should practice the disciplines of virtue which lead to self-control through right action and righteous living. In this manner, one's speech becomes *maakHeru* or truth. When one's speech becomes truth one's consciousness is truth. When one's consciousness is truth it is in harmony with the transcendental truth of the universe, which is symbolized by the Ancient Egyptian goddess MAAT. Thus, becoming true of speech is a primary goal for every spiritual aspirant since it is synonymous with coming into harmony with the universe and spiritual enlightenment.

Speaking the truth is an important spiritual art and should be used wisely and compassionately. Those who do not speak out against evil under the misguided notion that non-violence means no conflict are also part of the negativity. Speaking out is an expression of spiritual strength and wisdom which do not require violence and negativity. Emotionalism and animosity are hindrances to good speech. Speaking is an art to be performed when it will do the most good and not for idle talk or for showing off to others or to those who do not wish to listen. Speaking the truth should not be used when it will only serve to hurt people. A person becomes weak when they are constantly chasing after the egoistic desires. Therefore, spiritual strength and will power to resist and fight against injustice and violence increases when there is self-control, inner peace and self-discovery.

Speaking out is an expression of spiritual strength and wisdom which do not require violence

Meditation in the Discipline of Maat Philosophy

"Searching for one's self in the world is the pursuit of an illusion."

Egyptian Proverb

When the yoga of wisdom in action is perfected there is an intensification in your awareness of every thought and feeling which courses through the mind. Every single action which you perform or contemplate and every single perception that enters the mind is at the forefront of your awareness. No longer are you blindly following the whims of your senses. No longer do you say or do things without thinking first. No longer are you a slave to the degraded thoughts and feelings of the mind and no longer do you feel compelled to run after the desires of the body. The imaginations and fancies of the mind with respect to objects and people are gradually reduced. No

The Path of Action and Enlightenment

longer will you pursue objects to make yourself happy. No longer will you search for happiness through relationships with others. No longer will you try to fulfill your needs through the world. Your heart will begin to expand beyond measure and your fulfillment will run over.

Worship or devotion to the divine and consciousness or wisdom in action are the two secure paths for the majority of people. For this reason the ancient sages enjoined various deities or faces of the divine and various ethical precepts in order to allow the masses of people to develop spiritual sensitivity according to their capacity. The beauty of this teaching is that it is simple and available to everyone. Anyone may practice Maat while performing any action and wherever they may be. In the higher stages of practice the aspirant is led to develop identity with the divine with one-pointed concentration. When this occurs, there is an awakening of the mind from all of the lower states of consciousness into the transcendental state or Enlightenment.

Maat shows what is truth and what is illusion. Maat provides a higher ideal for human existence and the means to attain that higher goal. When the mind is trained to follow Maat, the impurities cause ignorance in the mind and which fetter the soul are destroyed. When the ignorance of the mind is rent asunder through the wisdom of Maat, the soul assumes its true nature, thereby transcending Maat and becoming one with the Divine. In this manner, once having done its cleansing work, soap is rinsed away along with the dirt, leaving purity alone in its original essence. In much the same way that soap is not the goal of cleanliness but a means to it, the wisdom of Maat is a means to unity with God. When the practice of Maat is perfected, the practice ceases and one becomes Maat.

When the ignorance of the mind is rent asunder through the wisdom of Maat, the soul assumes its true nature.

Part III: The 42 precepts of Maat

"MAAT, DAUGHTER OF RA"

The 42 Precepts of Maat are a condensation of the teachings of the Ancient Egyptian Wisdom Texts which were created by the ancient Egyptian sages. They form the basis of Kamitan society as well as the foundation of Shetaut Neter spirituality. Therefore, they are extremely important to the aspirant who wishes to practice the path of Maat (Divine Action) for they purify the heart and enable a human being to be qualified to aspire to higher teachings and spiritual realizations.

The following is a composite summary of "negative confessions" from several Ancient Egyptian *Books of Coming Forth by Day*. They are often referred to as "Negative Confessions" since the person uttering them is affirming what moral principles they have not transgressed. In this respect they are similar to the Yamas or ethical restraints of India. While all of these books include 42 precepts, some specific precepts varied according to the specific initiate for which they were prepared and the priests who compiled them. Therefore, I have included more than one precept per line where I felt it was appropriate to show that there were slight variations in the precepts and to more accurately reflect the broader view of the original texts.

Those who practice the following precepts and keep them foremost in their lives will attain the highest realization of Maat Philosophy. For more information on the practice of the 42 precepts see the book *The 42 Precepts of Maat and the Philosophy of Righteous Action* by Muata Ashby.

Hieroglyphic Text	Translation by Muata Ashby
(hieroglyphic text)	(1) "I have not done iniquity." Variant: Acting with falsehood.
	(2) "I have not robbed with violence."
	(3) "I have not done violence (To anyone or anything)." Variant: Rapacious (Taking by force; plundering.)
	(4) "I have not committed theft." Variant: Coveted.
	(5) "I have not murdered man or woman." Variant: Or ordered someone else to commit murder.
	(6) "I have not defrauded offerings." Variant: or destroyed food supplies or increased or decreased the measures to profit.
	(7) "I have not acted deceitfully." Variant: With crookedness.
	(8) "I have not robbed the things that belong to God."
	(9) "I have told no lies."
	(10) "I have not snatched away food."
	(11) "I have not uttered evil words." Variant: Or allowed myself to become sullen, to sulk or become depressed.
	(12) "I have attacked no one."
	(13) "I have not slaughtered the cattle that are set apart for the Gods." Variant: The Sacred bull – (Apis)
	(14) "I have not eaten my heart" (overcome with anguish and distraught). Variant: Committed perjury.
	(15) "I have not laid waste the ploughed lands."
	(16) "I have not been an eavesdropper or pried into matters to make mischief." Variant: Spy.
	(17) "I have not spoken against anyone." Variant: Babbled, gossiped.

The Path of Action and Enlightenment

(18) "I have not allowed myself to become angry without cause."

(19) "I have not committed adultery." Variant: And homosexuality.

(20) "I have not committed any sin against my own purity."

(21) "I have not violated sacred times and seasons."

(22) "I have not done that which is abominable."

(23) "I have not uttered fiery words. I have not been a man or woman of anger."

(24) "I have not stopped my ears against the words of right and wrong (Maat)."

(25) "I have not stirred up strife (disturbance)." "I have not caused terror." "I have not struck fear into any man."

(26) "I have not caused any one to weep." Variant: Hoodwinked.

(27) "I have not lusted or committed fornication nor have I lain with others of my same sex." Variant: or sex with a boy.

(28) "I have not avenged myself." Variant: Resentment.

(29) "I have not worked grief, I have not abused anyone." Variant: Quarrelsome nature.

(30) "I have not acted insolently or with violence."

(31) "I have not judged hastily." Variant: or been impatient.

(32) "I have not transgressed or angered God."

(33) "I have not multiplied my speech overmuch (talk too much).

(34) "I have not done harm or evil." Variant: Thought evil.

(35) "I have not worked treason or curses on the King."

(36) "I have never befouled the water." Variant: held back the water from flowing in

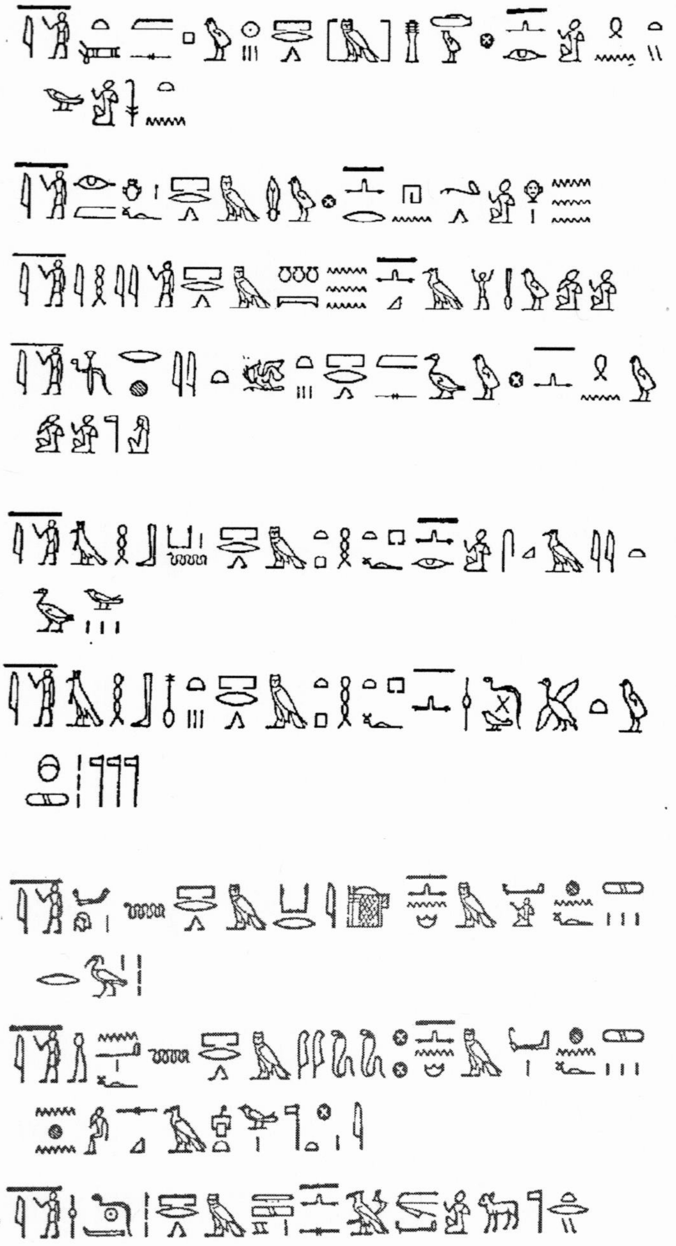

[Hieroglyphic text columns]

its season.

(37) "I have not spoken scornfully." <u>Variant: Or yelled unnecessarily or raised my voice.</u>

(38) "I have not cursed The God."

(39) "I have not behaved with arrogance." <u>Variant: Boastful.</u>

(40) "I have not been overwhelmingly proud or sought for distinctions for myself (Selfishness)."

(41) "I have never magnified my condition beyond what was fitting or increased my wealth, except with such things as are (justly) mine own possessions by means of Maat." <u>Variant: I have not disputed over possessions except when they concern my own rightful desired more than what is rightfully mine.possessions. Variant: I have not</u>

(42) "I have never thought evil (blasphemed) or slighted The God in my native town."

The Path of Action and Enlightenment

FOUNDATIONS OF MAAT PHILOSOOPHY

MAAT-UBUNTU: Maat Philosophy of Ancient Africa and Humanism in Present Day African Religious Practice

After centuries of trying to stop the practice of African Religion and convert Africans to Christianity, the Catholic Church reversed itself and at the 1964 Vatican II conference of Bishops in Rome, officially accepted African Religion into the family of World religions as a full partner.[20] On a visit to Benin, Pope John Paul II apologized for centuries of denigration African religion by the Western Culture. African religion is universally accepted as a distinct and legitimate form of spirituality and continues to be practiced by a substantial number of people in and outside of Africa. It is practiced by many who on one hand profess to be converts to Western religions while at the same time retain the practice of some aspects of African religion in their life. One reason for its persistence is the quality of *Humanism* that characterizes it. The African term *Ubuntu* means humanism. Humanism is a fundamental concern for the human condition, a caring for fellow human beings with respect to their well being, but also it means a kind of openness, hospitality and compassion for those in need. The quality of Ubuntu has had the effect of tempering the harshness of other religions, as well as bringing to the forefront the sufferings and needs of others, and sometimes the inequities that are endured by others. Ubuntu is a kind of empathy and sympathy for others and a heartfelt desire to share with others. One important example of the effect of African religion and its quality of Ubuntu is the Aldura Church of Yoruba. In this church the Christian emphasis on salvation has given way to an approach that is more in line with the traditional needs of the people. The priests function as diviners, healers and ritual leaders. The concept of humanism may be best expressed in the following quotations:

> "African belief is basically the humanistic belief that doing good is good, while doing anything bad is bad. You are rewarded here on earth for your good deeds and punished for your iniquities. Indeed, many

Pope John Paul II apologized for centuries of denigration African religion by the Western Culture.

---

[20] *African Religion: World Religion* by Aloysius M. Lugira

Introduction To MAAT PHILOSOPHY

Africans believe that the ultimate punishment for bad or iniquitous behaviour is death."

-N. Adu Kwabena-Essem is a freelance journalist, based in Accra, Ghana

"You know when it is there, and it is obvious when it is absent. It has to do with what it means to be truly human, it refers to gentleness, to compassion, to hospitality, to openness to others, to vulnerability, to being available for others and to know that you are bound up with them in the bundle of life, for a person is only a person through other persons."

-South Africa's Archbishop Desmond Tutu, winner of the Nobel Prize 1984

When compared to the concept of Ubuntu, the Kamitan concept of Ari Maat (Maatian Actions) is found to be in every way compatible with this concept of humanism or social awareness and caring. Maat is a philosophy, a spiritual symbol as well as a cosmic energy or force which pervades the entire universe. Maat is the path to promoting world order, justice, righteousness, correctness, harmony and peace. Maat is also the path that represents wisdom and spiritual awakening through balance and equanimity, as well as righteous living and selfless service to humanity. So Maat encompasses certain disciplines of right action which promote purity of heart and balance of mind. Maat is represented as a goddess with a feather held to the side of her head by a bandana and she is sometimes depicted with wings, a papyrus scepter in one hand and holding an ankh (symbol of life) in her other hand.

> Maat encompasses certain disciplines of right action which promote purity of heart and balance of mind.

Forms of Goddess Maat

In Kamit, the judges were initiated into the teachings of MAAT, for only when there is justice and fairness in society can there be an abiding harmony and peace. Harmony and peace are necessary for the pursuit of true happiness and inner fulfillment in life. Thus, Kamitan spirituality includes a discipline for social order and harmony not unlike Confucianism of China or Dharma of India. Maat promotes social harmony and personal virtue which lead to spiritual enlightenment.

Many people are aware of the 42 Laws or Precepts of Maat. They are declarations of purity (also known as *negative confessions)*, found in the Kamitan Book of Enlightenment (Egyptian Book of the Dead), which a person who has lived a life of righteousness can utter at the time of the great judgment after death. All of the precepts concern moral rectitude in all aspects of life which leads to social order. Order leads to prosperity and harmony.

As an adjunct to the 42 precepts there are other injunctions given in the Wisdom Texts. These in turn are elaborated in the tomb inscriptions of Ancient Egypt. In Chapter 125 of the Book of the Dead, the person uttering the declarations states:

> "I have done God's will. I have given bread to the hungry, water to the thirsty, clothes to the clotheless and a boat to those who were shipwrecked. I made the prescribed offerings to the gods and goddesses and I also made offerings in the temple to the glorious spirits. Therefore, protect me when I go to face The God."[21]

The following tomb inscriptions were carved into the walls of those people who professed to have lived a righteous and orderly life. Central to this order and virtue are the acts of righteousness and the highest form of right action is selfless service. That is, all of the things a person can do to uphold truth, order and righteousness during their lives. The following is a summary of Ari Maat, which will be followed by a brief gloss on Maat Selfless Service.

The Actions of a Person Living by Maat Should Include:

❶

Nuk rdy maat - *Give righteousness, order and truth to humanity*

Maat is the ancient art of ethical conduct, righteous living (virtue) and truth. Aspirants learn to think and act with honesty, integrity, and truthfulness to promote positive self-development which will translate into the becoming reliable and responsible leaders and members of society.

❷

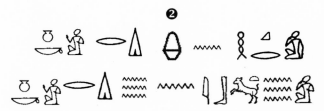

Nuk rdy ta n heker - Nuk rdy mu n abt
Give food to the hungry - Give water to the thirsty

Sharing food and drink are primary ways of showing compassion and promoting caring between human beings and societies.

Working to eradicate hunger and thirst in our community, and also world hunger, should be primary goals of a person living by Maat. Hunger prevents humanity from achieving its higher goals of peace and harmony. Hunger is a source of suffering and early death for millions of people around the world. Sharing food and drink are primary ways of showing compassion and promoting caring between

---

[21] For the full text see the *Book of the Dead* by Muata Ashby

human beings and societies. This promotes peace and prevents conflicts.

❸

Nuk rdy het n an het
Give shelter to the homeless

Working to provide homes for the homeless and alleviating the homeless situation in society should be a priority for a person living by Maat because all human beings require a proper place to dwell so that they can live well ordered and comfortable lives. Lack of shelter gives rise to discomfort and discomfort leads to strife.

❹

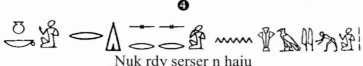

Nuk rdy serser n haiu
Give comfort to the weepers (suffering-disheartened)

Pain and suffering are all too prevalent in human life. One of the concerns of a person living by Maat should be to promote compassion and consolation to people who are suffering due to any reason and to promote immediate psychological support (refuge, moral support) for those in need.

❺

Nuk rdy netu genu kher nekhtu
Give protection to the weak from the strong

One of the main concerns of a person living by Maat should be social justice, the protection of the weaker members of society who are victims of crime or who are less able to help themselves when confronted with other members of society. The goal is to assist people by standing with them to provide moral, legal or other assistance.

❻

Nuk rdy rech n kheman
Give wisdom (counsel) to the ignorant

One of the main goals of a person living by Maat should be to train other human beings in the precepts of Maat and raise leaders who will study the ancient philosophy and be able to transmit it to others in society. This will promote the formation and growth of a well-informed segment of the population who will be able to promote peace, justice, understanding and spiritual enlightenment.

The Path of Action and Enlightenment

❼

Nuk rdy dept n an dept
Give opportunity to the discouraged

Having become wise and acting with virtue, teaching the ancient Maat Philosophy and assisting others in immediate and long-term need, a person living by Maat will thereby eventually assist them to become stronger and help themselves. Every human being needs to have the opportunity to develop and discover the meaning of life so as to grow and develop to their full potential. Therefore, justice and equal opportunity are essential human concerns for all people.

Maat Selfless Service is an important aspect of Chapter 33 (125) of the Book of the Dead. Here the initiate states {his/her} qualifications to be allowed into the inner shrine to see and become one with Asar (The Supreme Being). The initiate states that {he/she} helped those in need in various ways. This is one of the greatest and most secure methods of purifying the heart (becoming virtuous), because it makes one humble and it effaces the ego. Selfless Service is a vast area of spiritual practice and it forms the major part of the Yogic Path of Right Action. Every human being needs to understand the profound implications of selfless service and how to practice selfless service effectively in order to attain spiritual enlightenment, social order and harmony.

This is one of the greatest and most secure methods of purifying the heart

First it must be understood that according to Maat Philosophy, the Supreme Spirit (God, Goddess) manifests as all Creation, and is also present in all human beings. This being so, one must realize that one is interacting in, with and through the Supreme Spirit in all actions, speech and thought. Since human interrelations have a most profound influence on the human mind, they are the most powerful means of effecting a change in the personality. However, if mishandled, they can be a most effective method of leading a human being to psychological attachment and suffering as well. A person should understand that Maat comes to {him/her} in the form of human beings in need, so as to give the aspirant an opportunity to grow spiritually through selfless service. To be successful in selfless service, the aspirant must be able to sublimate the ego through developing patience, dealing with difficult personalities without developing resentment, not taking attacks personally, and developing a keen understanding of human nature and human needs. Selfless Service allows a human being to discover sentiments of caring for something greater than the little "me." This leads to purity of heart from the gross fetters of anger, hatred, greed, lust, jealousy, envy, etc., and also the attachments based on blood relations and other filial relationships, for in order to serve in the highest order, one must serve all equally, without favorites. As a servant of humanity, one's family becomes all human beings and nature itself. Therefore, the cause of environmental well being is also a high concern reflected in the following injunctions of the Maat philosophy. There are two injunctions that specifically address issues of public or selfless service to the community through service to nature and the preservation of natural resources.

(15) "I have not laid waste the ploughed lands."
(36) "I have never befouled the water." Variant: I have not held back the water from flowing in its season.

Introduction To MAAT PHILOSOPHY

—From Chapter 33 of the Ancient Egyptian Pert M Heru

When asked how she could stand to serve such severely ill people and not feel disheartened, repulsed or depressed, Mother Teresa replied "I see only Jesus coming to me through people." This reply shows the saintly attitude towards humanity, and she also displayed the highest level of spiritual practice through the path of right action, which is known as Selfless Service. When Mother Teresa was asked how she is able to do all the work she has done, she would reply, "I do nothing…God does it all." Selfishness arises when a human being sees {him/her} self as separate from Creation and develops an egoistic selfishness, typified by the attitude of "I got mine you get yours." A mature and righteous person must develop sensitivity to the fact that all Creation is inexorably linked at all levels, the material and the spiritual, and therefore, a true aspirant feels empathy and compassion for all humanity and will not rest until all human beings have the essential needs of life, those being food, shelter and opportunity to grow and thrive. All problems of the world can be traced to the selfishness and hoarding of precious basic necessities by certain segments of the population, and the subsequent development of resentments, greed, hatred and violence which lead to untold social strife.

However, a person who lives by Maat does not pursue the betterment of the world in a sentimental manner, but with deep understanding of the fact that people's ignorance of their true divine essence is the root cause that has led them to their current condition of suffering, and therefore simply sending money or aid will not resolve the issue. Where food, clothing or funds are needed, they should be given, but in addition to these, one must undertake an effort to promote mystical spiritual wisdom (which includes the complete practice of religion: myth, ritual and mysticism) in humanity. Beyond the basic necessities of life, the world needs mystical spiritual wisdom most of all. Technology, comforts of life, entertainments and other conveniences should come later. This is how a well-ordered society is structured along Maatian-Ubuntu principles: Mystical spiritual foundation which provides basic necessities (food and shelter) for its members, from which all else (development of technology, entertainment, etc.) will follow. Only in this way will the technological developments, entertainment and other aspects of society develop in a righteous (ethical), balanced and harmonious way. This can be contrasted with the current predicament of most modern day societies where the emphasis is foremost on the development of technology and entertainment, without giving much thought to spirituality (ethics, balance, harmony, truth, righteousness). Consequently, there are many people currently existing in communities all over the world who are deprived of the basic needs of life (food and shelter).

Studying the teachings of maat mysticism and their subsequent practice through selfless service will promote the enlightenment of humanity, which will end the cycle of egoism and disharmony between peoples of differing cultures. Therefore, the act of helping others is extremely important and should be pursued by all. Working in service of other human beings allows a person who lives by Maat to apply the teachings and experience the results. It allows the a person who lives by Maat to develop the capacity to adapt and adjust to changing conditions of life, and to other personalities, and still maintain the detachment and poise necessary to keep equal vision and awareness of the Divine, and thereby live by truth, and not by favoritism. All of this promotes integration of the personality of the person who lives by Maat.

The act of helping others is extremely important and should be pursued by all.

The Path of Action and Enlightenment

Therefore, the results of one's selfless service actions are immediate and always good, because no matter what the results of those actions are, the service itself is the goal of a person who lives by Maat.

What are the disciplines of Selfless Service?

Service is an important ingredient in the development of spiritual life. In selfless service one adopts the attitude of seeing and serving the Divine in everyone and every creature, and one is to feel as an instrument of the Divine, working to help the less able. The following are some important points to keep in mind when practicing selfless service.

First, having controlled the body, speech and thoughts, a person who lives by Maat should see {him/her} self as an instrument of the Divine, being used to bring harmony, peace, and help to the world. All human beings and nature are expressions of the Divine. Serving human beings and nature is serving the Supreme Divine Self (God).

In Chapter 34, Verse 10 of the Pert M Hru scripture, the initiate states that {he/she} has become a spiritual doctor: There are sick, very ill people. I go to them, I spit on the arms, I set the shoulder, and I cleanse them. As a servant of the Divine Self, a person who lives by Maat is also a healer. Just as it would be inappropriate for a medical doctor to lose {his/her} patience with {his/her} patient because the person is complaining due to their illness, so too it is inappropriate for an initiate to lose their patience when dealing with the masses of worldly-minded people, suffering from the illness of ignorance of their true essence. So, it must be clearly and profoundly understood that in serving, you are serving the true Self, not the ego.

Secondly, as discussed above, a person who lives by Maat should not expect a particular result from their actions. In other words one does not perform actions and wait for a reward or praises, and though working to achieve success in the project, one does not develop the expectation that one's efforts will succeed, because there may be failure in what one is trying to accomplish. If a person who lives by Maat focuses on the success of the project and failure occurs, the mind will become so imbalanced that it will negate the positive developments of personality integration, expansion and concentration which occurred as the project was pursued. Therefore, one's focus should be on doing one's part by performing the service, and letting the Divine handle the results. This provides a person who lives by Maat with peace and the ability to be more qualitative in the work being performed (without the egoistic content), and more harmonious, which will lead to being more sensitive to the needs of others and of the existence of the Spirit as the very essence of one's being.

one's focus should be on doing one's part by performing the service

Introduction To MAAT PHILOSOPHY

Secular Maat Selfless Service Leads to Spiritual Maat Mysticism

The highly advanced and lofty teachings from Maat Philosophy of becoming one with the Supreme Being through righteous action is further augmented by the Hymn to Maat contained in the scripture now referred to as the Berlin papyrus below.

Maat Ankhu Maat
Maat is the source of life
Maat neb bu ten
Maat is in everywhere you are
Cha hena Maat
Rise in the morning with Maat
Ankh hena Maat
Live with Maat
Ha sema Maat
Let every limb join with Maat (i.e. let her guide your actions)
Maat her ten
Maat is who you are deep down (i.e. your true identity is one with the Divine)
Dua Maat neb bu ten
Adorations to goddess Maat, who is in everywhere you are!

For more extensive study of the Maat-Selfless Service teaching, see the books 42 Precepts of Maat *and* Ancient Egyptian Book of the Dead *by Muata Ashby.*

The Path of Action and Enlightenment

The Supreme Offering of Maat

In the practice of Maat philosophy the sages have declared that the highest offering a person can make is the practice of Maat in day to day life. Even the kings and queens symbolically offer a figure of Maat to their chosen divinity as proof of their upholding of Maat (righteousness and justice) for all members of society and the temple. This means performing selfless service as well as living by the precepts of Maat in ones personal life.

Plate 5: The Offering of Maat-Symbolizing the Ultimate act of Righteousness (Temple of Seti I) The King offers to Asar (not pictured).

One of the main duties of the king is to uphold Maat. Maat is the ethical basis for harmonious social order. It is also the duty of the king to protect Maat by opposing all who seek to destroy peace and justice. The highest expression of the king's pledge to uphold Maat is to make the "Maat Offering."

The offering of the Maat

The King offering the Eye

- **Maat Offering:** By acting with righteousness and attaining virtue the supreme offering is made through the Maat Offering in which the person making the offering enters into a meditative awareness through the ritual and sees {him/her} self as becoming one with Maat.

Introduction To MAAT PHILOSOPHY

Chapter 125 of The Book of Coming Forth By Day and The Wisdom Texts

The Wisdom Texts are Ancient Egyptian writings which extol the virtue of righteous living and the idea of righteous living as a path to spiritual enlightenment. The main purpose of the texts is to instruct in the art of living which leads to peace and harmony in life and spiritual emancipation through effacement of the ego and devotion to God.

Though the Ancient Egyptian *Book of Coming Forth By Day* is the most popular text of Ancient Egypt it must be understood that the *Wisdom Texts* are the source of the teachings presented in the *Book of Coming Forth By Day*. The teachings expressed in the *Book of Coming Forth By Day* known as the 42 precepts of Maat are in reality a culmination or an affirmation of a life lived according to righteous conduct and spiritual wisdom. The *Wisdom Texts* date back to the period of 5,000 B.C.E. known as the "Old Kingdom" period of Dynastic Egypt and represent the earliest known examples of instructions in the art of living for harmony in society and for spiritual evolution. They were copied upon papyruses and were designed for the general instruction of the Ancient Egyptian population.

In Chapter 125 of the Ancient Egyptian *Book of Coming Forth By Day* it is stated that one should be able to declare one's innocence from wrong doing in order to see the face of God. How is this possible? Can a human being aspire to perfection and divine vision? The Wisdom Texts show how this is possible in language and instructions which are relevant to modern times. The teachings are universal and therefore applicable to all human beings regardless of the country of origin, the religious affiliation, the gender, the age, etc.

> The teachings are universal and therefore applicable to all human beings.

Through the practice of the precepts of Maat mental peace and subtlety of intellect (purity of heart) arise. Purity of heart, meaning the absence or anger, hatred, greed, jealousy, discontent, covetousness, elation, stress, agitation, etc. is the means through which divine awareness is possible. When the mind is beset with agitation it is impossible to develop spiritual sensitivity. The mind in this state is as if caught in a web of illusion based on the thoughts, desires and ignorance which do not allow awareness of the Divine essence within the heart or in nature, but rather intensify the feelings of individualism, separation and individuality. These in turn open the door for feelings egoistic or personal desires to arise. Feelings of animosity, anger, hatred, greed, jealousy, lust, elation, depression, etc. can only exist when there is individuality or egoism.

Think about it, can you feel jealous of your arm, your head, your foot? No because these are part of you, they are an integral part of your being. In the same way, a perfected (righteous) Sage or Saint sees the entire universe as his or her body and therefore cannot feel jealous, angry, greedy, etc. towards anything or anyone. This is because the feeling of ignorance, individuality and separation has been replaced with truth and universality. There is equal vision towards all and universal love for all that exists. This is the experience of an enlightened human being.

The Path of Action and Enlightenment

The *Wisdom Texts* are to be read, chanted or written daily. This is especially true of chapter 125 of *Book of Coming Forth By Day*. In this manner they are to be studied and practiced so as to engender a mind that is peaceful and harmonious. The following is a rendition of Chapter 125 of the *Book of Coming Forth of Ani.*

THE TEACHINGS FOR ENTERING INTO THE HALL OF MAATI TO PRAISE ASAR KHENTI-AMENTI.

The Asar the scribe Ani, whose word is truth, saith:-
I have come unto thee.
I have drawn nigh to behold thy beauties (thy beneficent goodness).
My hands are [extended] in adoration of thy name of "Maat."
I have come. I have drawn close unto [the place where] the cedar-tree existeth not, where the acacia tree does not put forth shoots, and where the ground produceth neither grass nor herbs.
Now I have entered into the habitation which is hidden, and I hold converse with Set.
My protector advanced to me, covered was his face.... on the hidden things.
He entered into the house of Asar, he
saw the hidden things which were therein. The Tchatchau Chiefs of the Pylons were in the form of Spirits.
The god Anpu spake unto those about him with the words of a man who cometh from Ta-mera, saying, "He knoweth our roads and our towns.
I am reconciled unto him.
When I smell his odor it is even as the odor of one of you."
And I say unto him: I the Asar Ani, whose word is truth, in peace, whose word is truth, have come.
I have drawn close to behold the Great Gods.
I would live upon the propitiatory offerings [made] to their Doubles.
I would live on the borders [of the territory of] the Soul, the Lord of Tetu.
He shall make me to come forth in the form of a Benu bird, and to hold converse [with him.]
I have been in the stream [to purify myself].
I have made offerings of incense.
I betook myself to the Acacia Tree of the [divine] Children. I lived in Abu in the House of the goddess Satet.
I made to sink in the water the boat of the enemies.
I sailed over the lake [in the temple] in the Neshmet Boat.
I have looked upon the Sahu of Kamur.
I have been in Tetu.
I have held my peace.
I have made the god to be master of his legs.
I have been in the House of Teptuf.
I have seen him, that is the Governor of the Hall of the God. I have entered into the House of Asar and I have removed the head-coverings of him that is therein.
I have entered into Rasta, and I have seen the Hidden One who is therein.
I was hidden, but I found the boundary.

Introduction To MAAT PHILOSOPHY

I journeyed to Nerutef, and he who was therein covered me with a garment.

I have myrrh of women, together with the shenu powder of living folk.

Verily he (Asar) told me the things which concerned himself.

I said: Let thy weighing of me be even as we desire.

And the Majesty of Anpu shall say unto me, "Knowest thou the name of this door, and can thou tell it?" And the Asar the scribe Ani, whose word is truth, in peace, whose word is truth, shall say,

"Khersek-Shu" is the name of this door. And the Majesty of the god Anpu shall say unto me, "Knowest thou the name of the upper leaf, and the name of the lower leaf?" [And the Asar the scribe Ani] shall

say: "Neb-Maat-heri-retiu-f" is the name of the upper leaf and "Neb-pehti-thesu-menment" [is the name of the lower leaf. And the Majesty of the god Anpu shall say], "Pass on, for thou hast knowledge, O Asar the scribe, the assessor of the holy offerings of all the gods of Thebes Ani, whose word is truth, the lord of loyal service [to Asar]."

*The next pages contain the affirmations of internal purity otherwise known as the "Negative Confessions"

The Path of Action and Enlightenment

RUBRIC: THE MAKING OF THE REPRESENTATION OF
WHAT SHALL HAPPEN IN
THIS HALL OF MAATI.

This Chapter shall be recited or chanted by the spiritual aspirant when he is cleansed and purified, and is arrayed in linen apparel, and is shod with sandals of white leather, and his eyes are painted with antimony, and his body is anointed with unguent made of myrrh. And he shall present as offerings oxen, and feathered fowl, and incense, and cakes and ale, and garden herbs. And behold, thou shalt draw a representation of this in color upon a new tile molded from earth upon which neither a pig nor any other animal hath trodden. And if this book be done [in writing, the deceased] shall flourish, and his children shall flourish, and [his name] shall never fall into oblivion, and he shall be as one who fills the heart of the king and of his princes. And bread, and cakes, and sweetmeats, and wine, and pieces of flesh shall be given unto him [from among those which are] upon the altar of the Great God. And he shall not be driven back from any door in Amentet, and he shall be led along with the kings of the South and the kings of the North, and he shall be in the company of Asar, continually and regularly for ever. [And he shall come forth in every form he pleaseth as a living soul for ever, and ever, and ever.]

This Teaching is effective a million times...

SUMMATION OF THE PRECEPTS OF MAAT

The 42 declarations of purity have profound implications for the spiritual development of the individual as well as for society. They may be grouped under three basic ethical teachings, *Truth, Non-violence* and *Self-Control.* Under the heading of self-control, three subheadings may be added, *Balance of Mind or Right Thinking Based on Reason, Non-stealing* and *Sex-Sublimation.*

Truth 1, 6, 8, 15, 18, 22, 26, 27, 34

Non-violence 2, 4, 5, 10 , 12, 14, 23, 25, 29, 33,

Self-Control-Right Action 10, 16, 17, 22, 24, 25, 28, 31, 32, 35, 37, 39

   Balance of Mind-reason, 13, 19, 26, 30, 36, 38,

   Not-stealing 3, 6, 7, 9, 40, 41, 42

   Sex-Sublimation 11, 20, 21

Introduction To MAAT PHILOSOPHY

THE PATH OF NON-VIOLENCE

We have explored many dimensions of the theme of non-violence in the precepts of Maat (2, 4, 5, 10 , 12, 14, 23, 25, 29, 33,) as well as throughout the Instructions of Merikara. Also, the main theme of another wisdom text, the Precepts of Ptahotep, deal with this issue exclusively.

Here the goal is to explore the deeper aspects of non-violence. This can be done by understanding the deep roots of violence and in so doing be able to root them out of the human personality. As stated earlier, violence arises out of ignorance but how does this ignorance manifest and how does it lead to violence?

Consider the teachings which have been presented in Ancient Egyptian Mysticism as well as in all major religions and mystical philosophies from around the world. The central theme is that all life, all existence is indeed part of one whole, one essence, one being. If this is true then everything is related to everything else like a family member. So why is it that people fail to see the connection? It is due to ignorance born of selfish desires. With this understanding the definition of violence must be reinterpreted so that we may understand the heart of the problems of human violence.

The development in spirituality can only occur when a spiritual aspirant allows his or her life to be permeated with truth, justice, correctness, wisdom and righteousness. Righteousness is any activity or movement which leads to self-discovery. Every aspect of life must be placed under the control of the teachings of righteousness, even when the ego is hurt or disappointed by the results.

The human ego often judges what is good by what pleases it. Therefore, anything that comes in the way of the desires of the ego is considered bad or evil. This feeling leads to anger and anger leads to hatred and violence. Feelings and thoughts of anger, hatred and violence constitute a human condition of vice. Vice leads to actions which are disharmonious and these create repercussions which ultimately bring negative results (more anger, hatred and violence) back to the person who originally expressed those feelings and actions. This is the cyclical movement in vice. Therefore, the wisdom teachings warn against thinking, feeling, acting with vice and associating with those who are controlled by their vices.

So one who is practicing virtue must understand that even though an activity may seem pleasurable to the ego, it may not be good for promoting a movement in virtue. Examples of this idea abound throughout the Wisdom Texts. While it may seem good to acquire something by lying, in the end, unrighteousness brings pain and sorrow. Along with this there is another important point. There is always a witness to a crime. God is the eternal watcher (Amun) who makes sure that a person never escapes from the repercussions of their actions. This is the Divine law of Ari, presided over by goddess Meskhenet, better known in modern times as the law of Karma.

Negative occurrences happen in life according to the cycle of vice based on a persons actions (karma). Underlying the cycle of vice is ignorance of the true Self. The movement in vice works in a manner such as is illustrated below.

> The human ego often judges what is good by what pleases it.

The Path of Action and Enlightenment

THE CYCLE OF VICE

Violence

↑

Anger and Hatred

↑

Frustration

↑

Negative Actions

↑

Greed, Passion, Weak Will, Irrationality

↑

Desire

↑

IGNORANCE

The root cause of vice in the human personality is ignorance of one's true identity as being one with the Self (God). Otherwise there would be no desire to acquire objects and no need to hate what obstructs one's movement to acquire what one desires or a need to love and become attached to what seems to bring pleasure because in self-knowledge there is peace, contentment and fulfillment. Without self-knowledge (the state of ignorance) there is always something missing, always a need to seek fulfillment. These needs give rise to the myriad forms of desire which arise in the human heart. The deep-rooted desires of the human heart wear down a human being's ability to act with reason and righteousness. The will is weakened and negative actions become accepted and sanctioned by the weak will. This was first understood and explained in the Wisdom Text writings known as "TEACHINGS OF PTAHOTEP":

The deep-rooted desires of the human heart wear down a human being's ability to act with reason and righteousness.

The fool who does not hear,
He can do nothing at all;
He sees knowledge in ignorance,
Usefulness in harmfulness.
He does all that one detests.

Epilog-Line 575
(circa 5,000 B.C.E. Ancient Egypt)

Introduction To MAAT PHILOSOPHY

THE MOVEMENT OF VIRTUE

If a man says: "I shall be rich,"
He will have to say: "My cleverness has snared me."
If he says: "I will snare for myself,"
He will be unable to say: "I snared for my profit.
If a man says: "I will rob someone,"
He will end being given to a stranger.
People's schemes do not prevail,
God's command is what prevails;
Live then in the midst of peace,
What they give comes by itself.

-From The Teachings of Ptahotep

The scripture above illustrates the futility of desires and the uselessness of engaging in vicious activities - based on anger, hatred, greed and so on. The desire for wealth and the scheming which it engenders in the mind is only a snare for the very same person who is desiring because this leads them to endless worldly entanglements and unforeseen situations wherein they will experience unrest and dissatisfaction. Thus, it is better to live life in harmony with the world, content to know that whatever is needed will be achieved as per the plan of God (What they give comes by itself.). This means that you should work for what is good according to the teachings of righteousness and then allow God to provide the results, or the fruits of your work according to your needs. This teaching of how to attain peace (spiritual realization) by renouncing desire for the results (fruits) of one's actions is similar in most respects to the instructions presented in the Ancient Hindu text: The Bhagavad Gita:

The desire for wealth and the scheming.

Gita: Chapter 2
Samkhya Yogah--The Yoga of Knowledge

41. O Delighter of the race of _Kuru_ (Arjuna), the intellect that ascertains the nature of the Self is one-pointed, but the thoughts of one who desires the fruits of action are many-branched and endless.

Gita: Chapter 5
Karma Sanyas Yoga--The Yoga of Renunciation of Action

12. One who is devoted to Yoga (Karma Yoga) attains peace by renouncing the fruits of action. But one who is not united with karma Yoga is impelled by desires, attached to the fruits of action, and therefore, goes to bondage.

Gita: Chapter 12
Bhakti Yogah--The Yoga of Devotion

12. Knowledge (indirect) is better than repeated effort (Abhyasa), and better than knowledge is Dhyana or meditation. From meditation follows renunciation of fruits of action, and from renunciation there arises ceaseless peace.

The movement of virtues is the path of the Practice of Yoga: Listening to the teachings, Reflection upon and practicing them in everyday life, and Meditation or intensified understanding and feeling toward the Divine and detachment towards the transient world of ordinary human experience. The practices of Yoga gradually cause a transformation in a human being which leads him or her from ignorance to Spiritual Enlightenment as follows.

Spiritual Enlightenment
↑
Experience of the Divine
↑
Faith
↑
Ignorance

The plan of spiritual evolution, presented above, will be easily seen as we move through the Wisdom Text known as *The Instructions To Merikara*. The numbers preceding each paragraph of the commentary will correspond to the line in the Wisdom Text.

For the *The Instructions To Merikara* see the section: "The Concept of Action and Fate in Maat Philosophy"

The diagram above may be further also understood as follows:

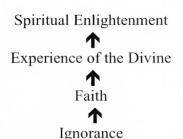

Spiritual Enlightenment and Immortality
↑
Peace
↑
Happiness
↑
Inner Fulfillment
↑
Self-Control and Contentment
↑
UNDERSTANDING

Understanding relates to the process of Yoga: Listening, Reflection and Meditation on the teachings)

If all Creation is one whole and you are part of that whole then what do you own? Do you own a house, car, television, a plot of land? No you cannot own anything. You are just a passing caretaker on your journey through this particular lifetime. So then why do you hoard things? Why do you proudly and egoistically display your possessions for all to see and why do you flaunt your possessions before those who are less fortunate? This is not only ignorant but violent. It is hurting others and it is in complete contradiction with the teachings of Maat. When you acquire land and say that you own it and you do not take care to protect the right of others to have land or even take measures to prevent "those people" from living close to you or from getting ahead in life you are doing as much violence as a common street thug. The resentment and animosity that this kind of violence brings is explained by people in an arrogant and selfish way: "If they want something they can work hard like I had to," or "if they get equal opportunity there won't be enough for all of us so better that they should suffer than me and mine." These statements point to the deep roots of ignorance and egoism which translate from individuals to society and it is a primary cause of wars and other forms of social strife. So society suffers as a result of violence but individuals also suffer because when they engender anger and hatred in others that same anger is visited upon them as well in return, if not in this lifetime perhaps in the next. How you live your life determines your fate after death. So if you were selfish in life you will experience deprivation after death and the cause of your own destiny of negativity. Sharing is the cornerstone of peace and it is a supreme expression of love.

Maat is the one who provides the relentless order of the universe which allows the world with its land, water, air and fire to sustain human existence and it is Maat who provides these for the fortunate and less fortunate alike, without discrimination. We must understand that fortunate or unfortunate, prosperous or adverse conditions arise from ones own actions. This law of ari or karma is also sustained by Goddess Maat. Thus, those who are less fortunate today are so due to wrong actions of the past. However, everyone can turn around a negative situation if there is correct action in the present. Also, those who are prosperous today where not always prosperous. In this lifetime or a previous one they experienced adversity and so should develop humility and compassion. They should lend a helping hand as they would to their own kin because every human being, every plant, animal, stone, particle of air, etc. is exactly that, your kin. So eradicate the seeds of violence in your heart through humility, spiritual knowledge and selfless service to humanity. Do not allow your mind to entertain thoughts of greed. Place it in the service of some noble cause which will purify your heart and engender a spiritual movement which will lead to enlightenment, the spiritual resurrection.

This law of *ari* or karma is also sustained by Goddess Maat.

Non-violence also means speaking out against injustice while harming no one. It is an expression of your inner understanding of the oneness of humanity. No matter what violence you have participated in in the past you must realize that you have the potential to completely transform your personality if you eradicate the seeds of ignorance, anger, hatred and greed. There is no real criminal, only a soul which has become deluded into the idea of egoism and separation. Sin is an error to be corrected and not a blot which will haunt you for ever. Unrighteousness of the past can be counteracted with correctness and righteousness of the present. Therefore, begin today on the road to truth, non-violence, justice and peace by first listening to the teachings and then studying and practicing the teachings for the rest of your life.

The Path of Action and Enlightenment

LISTENING TO AND PRACTICING THE TEACHINGS

Injunctions 15, 26, and 30 from the negative confessions of the *Book of Coming Forth By Day* holds important instruction on the study and practice of Maat philosophy.

(26) *"I have not stopped my ears against the words of right and wrong."*

What does it mean to "stopped my ears against the words of right and wrong?" Have you ever prevented someone from telling you something you did not want to hear? For instance, at a party or other gathering, did anyone say something thoughtful, like "smoking is bad for you" or "life if fleeting, look what happened to George, he died suddenly," only to have another person tell them to be quiet and not to discuss such things at a joyous occasion? Another example is becoming resentful when someone points out something you have said or done which is wrong. This teaching is a follow-up to number (15) *"I am not a person who lives by deceiving others or myself."* As a spiritual aspirant you must listen to the voice of wisdom from wherever and whenever it may come. This is the only way to improve your character and understand yourself.

(30) *"I have not acted or judged hastily."*

If you are prejudiced even before someone speaks how can you learn? It is impossible. Your own ignorance which you are holding onto with your ego will lead you into unfathomable miseries. Therefore, listen whenever the truth is spoken and you will receive divine grace in the form of wisdom and spiritual realization. The following verse from the Teachings of Ptahotep bring to mind the ideal of listening and how it leads to divine realization.

> He who hears is beloved of god,
> He whom god hates does not hear.
> The heart makes of its owner a hearer or non-hearer,"
> Man's heart is his life-prosperity-health
> The hearer is one who hears what is said,
> He who loves to hear is one who does what is said.
> How good for a son to listen to his father,
> How happy is he to whom it is said:
> "The son, he pleases as a master of hearing."
> The hearer of whom this is said,
> He is well-endowed
> And honored by his father;
> His remembrance is in the mouth of the living,
> Those on earth and those who will be.

Therefore, if one listens to the teachings and "takes them to heart" by living them, they will lead to divine grace.

The heart (mind) is either the source of all prosperity, health, happiness and well being or it can be the source of pain, suffering and anguish. Therefore, if one listens to the teachings and "takes them to heart" by living them, then they will lead to divine grace (He who hears is beloved of god) and spiritual enlightenment because righteous living (listening to and living by the teachings of righteousness) leads to purity of heart (maak-Heru).

Introduction To MAAT PHILOSOPHY

EGOISM AND PRIDE

The most important obstacle to spiritual realization is egoism and pride is an expression of it. All of the injunctions refer to the need to eradicate egoism, ignorance, violence and desire in the heart and special emphasis is placed on egoism in injunctions 32 and 38,

> (32) "I have not multiplied my
> speech overmuch."

> (38) "I have not behaved with arrogance."

Injunction 32 implies a personality which is of an outgoing nature but in an exaggerated way. This personality is distracted and always agitated, looking for something to get into. This follows along with injunction (31) *"I have not been an eavesdropper."* The concern with events and objects outside of oneself is the main cause of distraction in the mind. Distraction is the main cause of inability to discover the spiritual self within. Egoism is thinking of oneself as the personality and it is fueled by the distracted tendencies of the mind. Distraction leads to ignorance. Pride and egoism go hand in hand with spiritual ignorance because when one has spiritual knowledge it is clear that all humanity, all Creation is an expression of God. How can there be hatred for or discrimination against any part of God? This is only possible when there is ignorance and egoism. When there is egoism there is always a desire to promote what one believes one desires at the exclusion of the desires of others. One believes that one is correct and above others. This conceit and arrogance prevents one from seeing any reality beyond the confines of ones own concepts and ideas, thus everyone else is wrong. Conceit and arrogance are exacerbated when a person receives praise from others due to some achievement or degree which they have attained. In the state of ignorance (egoism), people cannot handle either praise or censure properly. When there is praise the ego swells and when there is censure the ego begins to lash out with curses, hatred and violence.

Distraction leads to ignorance.

The descriptions given above are for the purpose of explaining the human predicament of spiritual ignorance. In this deluded state the mind leads itself to conflict and unrighteousness (Setian qualities) as opposed to righteousness, truth and peace (Maat). Setian behavior is a deviation from the truth and this deviation is caused by the delusion of ignorance. A deluded human being can engage in racism, sexism, murder, violence, arrogance, etc. while a person who has discovered their spiritual essence cannot harm anyone or anything in thought, word or deed or any other way. This is why spiritual aspirants are cautioned to follow the path of righteousness (Maat) even while they are in a state of ignorance because acting in a righteous manner purifies the negative elements in the mind which foster the seeds of ignorance and egoism. These elements are the fetters of the soul: fear, desires, jealousy, greed, passion, etc. Thus, the project of a spiritual aspirant who wants to tread the path of Maat is to work toward cleansing the fetters. This is accomplished by selfless action as described earlier in this volume and through attaining spiritual knowledge through the study of the teachings.

There is one important factor which is inherent in the precepts of Maat that must receive special mention. Many times when people are ignorant of the greater spiritual realities and caught up in the emotionality of human life they tend to look for something to blame for their miseries. They want to find a cause for the troubles of life and the easiest way to do this is to look around into the world and point to those factors around them which seem to affect them. In Chapter 125 the use of the word *nuk* ("I") is emphasized with a special connotation. The spiritual aspirant says continually "I have not...." He or she does not say "you have allowed me" or "the devil made me do it" or "I wanted to but I couldn't," etc.

There is a process of responsibility wherein the spiritual aspirant recognizes that he or she has the obligation to act righteously and in so doing to purify their own heart. Spiritual practice can succeed only when you assume responsibility for your actions, thoughts, words and feelings. If you constantly blame your adversities on others or on situations, etc. you will be living life according to ignorance and weakness. True spiritual strength comes from leaning upon the Self within for spiritual support and well being rather than upon external situations, people or objects.

Spiritual practice can succeed only when you assume responsibility for...

Thus within the teachings of MAAT can be found all of the important injunctions for living a life which promotes purity, harmony and sanctity. While these may be found in other spiritual traditions from around the world, seldom is the emphasis on non-violence and balance to be found. In Christianity Jesus emphasized non-violence and in Buddhism Buddha emphasized non-violence. These traditions recognized the power of non-violence to heal the anger and hatred within the aggressor as well as the victim and when this spiritual force is developed it is more formidable that any kind of physical violence. Therefore, anyone who wishes to promote peace and harmony in the world must begin by purifying every bit of negativity within themselves. This is the only way to promote harmony and peace in others. Conversely, if there is anger within you you are indeed promoting anger outside of yourself and your efforts will be unsuccessful in the end.

PERFECTION IN ACTION

Perfection, in mystical teaching, is perfect harmony. In terms of action and the path of Maat it implies a harmonious, balanced manner of living wherein their is a concordance between your desires and the events of the world, when there is no conflict or contradiction. In this state the feelings of a person and their desires flow spontaneously with nature and with whatever the necessities are for their duties in life. For example, suppose that you wanted to go to the park but it began to snow so much that you cannot get out of your house. Perfection in action would not be to mope about, cursing the snow and Mother Nature. It might be to use the opportunity to catch up on some work you need to do or to engage in some other, equally rewarding pastime such as reading. Suppose you expected to go away on vacation but the same morning you planned to leave a tree fell on your house and the damage will require the entire amount you planned to spend on your vacation. Perfection here would not be to grumble and complain about your misfortune but to bear your adversity with poise, knowing that God has caused this situation for a purpose and that there is no use in losing your mental balance over it.

Perfection in action is a graceful, fluid, effortless, way of life which moves with the world. While trying to achieve certain goals in life and while trying to gain certain results from your actions you should not depend on these for your inner fulfillment. With this attitude you will be surprised at how much you are able to accomplish because you have not wasted any time in anger or grief. Your actions will become highly qualitative and inspired, thus you will be highly successful in any endeavor due to your powers of concentration and inner strength. Along with this you will experience uninterrupted peace within which will carry you through the adversities of life.

THE PATH OF MAAT AS A SPIRITUAL DISCIPLINE

Those who desire to tread the path of Maat should allow their devotional feeling to flow toward the Divine Mother, Maat. You must begin to feel that your actions, thoughts and words are those of the Goddess. Place yourself in her hands and allow her loving hand to guide you. Feel that the adversity you have created for yourself will be overcome through the grace of Maat. See adversity as lessons from the Divine Mother and chant her name in adoration and praise as the very source of your strength and will to destroy what is ignorant and sinful within yourself so as to purify your heart. Chant thus:

"Om Maati am Maak-Heru"
(The Divine Self manifesting as Maati, grant that I become purified and enlightened)

You must strive to understand that your struggles have not come to you by accident just as your prosperity also has not come to you by accident. You need to understand that God, in the form of the Maat, is behind every situation in your life just as she is behind the relentless and perfect movement of the planets and stars. With this wisdom you need to develop a feeling of contentment within yourself and to avoid useless and negative expectations. People expect things out of life, not realizing that the world is not set up to pamper anyone's ego. You may expect things and work for things out of life but knowing that the Divine Mother will grant you what you need just as a good parent provided what a child needs. You may pray for material things and desire them but not all of your prayers will be answered because there is a higher intelligence that knows what is best for you. Therefore, as a spiritual aspirant you should surrender your egoistic will and your egoistic desires to the will of the Divine Self. When you do so you will realize that the tension, anxiety and stress you created by pressuring yourself was useless and destructive because it led you away from inner peace and did not allow you to have clarity of mind to see the way out of your situation. You must develop a balance, a harmony in your life, this is Maat. In this balance you will be able to "know" which direction to take in life. This is the guidance from the Divine Mother.

> You must develop a balance, a harmony in your life, this is Maat.

See yourself as an instrument in the hands of the Divine Mother. This can be done by putting down your ego whenever you detect its rise. Always choose to act with righteousness instead of egoism and know that you will be provided for and that you need not worry. Have you ever been in trouble and somehow, in a mysterious way, you were able to get out of it? This was not luck or chance, it was the grace of the Divine Mother. Devote yourself to selfless service in the name of the Goddess. You need not advertise why you are doing what you are doing. Simply help others at every opportunity as it arises while at the same time keeping company with virtuous people with high minded ideals.

Pray each morning that the Divine Self may use you to better the world. Pray that you be led to purity of heart, that your mind be cleansed of negativity (anger, hatred, jealousy, greed, anxiety, stress, dullness, insecurity, agitation, etc.) which is crippling your ability to discover divine bliss and happiness. As you do these things you will develop insight into your calling and when you discover it you will feel a deeper enjoyment from that work which can not be measured in a monetary sense. Righteous action, selfless service, meditation, study of the teachings, self-control, equanimity, harmony, peace, order, contentment and effacement of the ego are the liquor of Maat. A spiritual aspirant must surround him or herself with this divine nectar because it is the substance which leads to spiritual enlightenment, the realization of immortality and supreme bliss while still alive and in the life beyond.

The Path of Action and Enlightenment

KARMA AND REINCARNATION IN THE ANCIENT EGYPTIAN BOOK OF COMING FORTH BY DAY

The Judgment Scene: The Meskhenet (Karmic) Scales and the Hall of Judgment.

Appendix A Figure 1: The Judgment of the Heart of Ani, from the Funerary papyrus of Ani.

Far left, Ani enters the hall of Judgment. His heart (conscience) is being weighed by Anubis while the Divine principles Shai, Renenet and Meskhenet look on. Ani's soul and his destiny also look on while Anubis measures Ani's heart against the feather of Maat. At far right Djehuti records the result while the Monster Ammit, the Devourer of the Unjust, awaits the answer.

The hands of Djehuti (God of wisdom) are "SHAI" which means "destiny" and "RENENET" which means "Fortune and Harvest." The implication is that we reap (harvest) the result of our state of mind (heart). Our state of mind including our subconscious feelings and desires is weighed against cosmic order, Maat. If found to be at peace (Hetep) and therefore in accord with cosmic order (Maat) it will be allowed to join with the cosmos (Asar). Otherwise it will suffer the fate as dictated by it's own contents (mental state of unrest due to lingering desires) which will lead it to Ammit who will devourer the ego-personality and the soul will experience torments from demons until we learn our lessons or become strong enough through wisdom to know ourselves. Demons are negative cosmic energies it has allowed itself to come in contact with or mental anguish and torments we put ourselves through due to our own ignorance. Self-torment may be regret over some action or inaction while alive or a reluctance to leave because of a lingering desire to experience more earthly pleasure. Therefore, we control our own fate according to our own level of wisdom.

Demons are negative cosmic energies

Appendix A Figure 2: Following the judgment, Asar Ani is taken by the androgynous Heru (note the female-left breast) and introduced to a mummified Asar who holds the Flail, Crook and Was staffs and is enthroned in a shrine surmounted by a Hawk - Heru. Asar wears a crown symbolic of Upper and Lower Egypt and is assisted by Nebthet and Aset. When Ani reaches the shrine, he is justified and glorified as symbolized by the anointment *"grease cone"* on his head (see Anointed One), and kneels with upraised right arm, holding a Sekhem staff in the left. In front of him there is a table of offerings including flowers, fruit and a **khepesh** or "foreleg of ox". Above him there are vessels of wine, beer and oils, and at the topmost compartment of the register, there is another offering table with bread, cakes, a wreath and a **"set"** or duck.

After being judged and having been found to be worthy (pure of heart), Ani is led by Heru, the Lord of Heaven and Earth (Upper and Lower Egypt), who is Ani's own androgynous soul, to Asar who is Ani's higher self. Ani has acquired the spiritual strength (Sekhem) to become one with Asar and thus will join Asar in Amenta. Ani's offering of the **"khepesh and set"** (symbols of male and female principles) represents Ani's relinquishment of his earthly - dualistic consciousness. Thus Ani is offering his ego-consciousness so that he may realize his non-dualistic - all-encompassing cosmic higher self in Asar.

Ani's offering of the **"khepesh and set"**

Now Ani's name becomes Asar-Ani. The green Asar, who in this teaching assumes the role of the male aspect of NETER[22], being supported by Nebthet (death) and Aset (life), is the Supreme deity (Heru) representing *"that which is up there"*. In this aspect, the green Asar' mummified form represents neither existence nor non-existence, neither life nor death but that which lies beyond, the Life Force (green) which vivifies all things. He holds the power of leading one to absolute reality (Shepherd's Crook), the power to emanate Life Force (Was), and the power to separate the mortal human body from the eternal soul just as the winnowing whip or Flail separates the chaff from the seed. Aset and Nebthet (life and death) represent

---

[22] Other teachings concerning Asar describe an androgynous, omnipotent, hidden, all pervading being who supports all life. In various other texts, the same attributes are ascribed to Aset, Hathor, Heru, Amun, Ra, Ptah, and to other male and female Egyptian Creator divinities. Thus we are led to understand that there is one Supreme Being which is the basis of the Egyptian mysteries, in the same way as the Indian Gods and Goddesses Krishna, Rama, Brahma, Vishnu, Shiva, Saraswati, Kali, Parvati represent male and female aspects of the Supreme Divinity in Hindu mythology.

The Path of Action and Enlightenment

Creation for only in the realm of creation can there be "life" or "death". In the realm of Asar there is only eternal life. From the feet of Asar rises the World Lotus (symbol of creation) with the four sons of Heru (all directions of the compass - meaning all encompassing) standing on it. Asar wears the Atef crown which is composed of the Hadjet crown (Upper Egypt), the Double Plumes crown (Amun) and a small solar disk at the top (Ra) not shown in scene above.[23] Therefore, Asar incorporates the attributes of Heru, Amun and Ra. Thus, to join Asar in Amenta is to join with the attributes of Asar since Amenta is Asar. In this way one's own soul is responsible for its own fate, either to be led by Apep (ignorance) into the jaws of Ammit (destruction, suffering, reincarnation) or to union with Asar (Hetep-eternal peace). Thus, it is one's own enlightened soul (Heru) who leads one (Ani) to union with one's true self (Asar).

For more on the teachings of karma: Maat, Meskhenet, Djehuti, Shai and Rennenet see the books *The Book of the Dead* and *Resurrecting Osiris* by Dr. Muata Ashby.

I am pure. I am pure. I am Pure.

I have washed my front parts with the waters of libations,
I have cleansed my hinder parts with drugs which make wholly clean,
and my inward parts have been washed in the liquor of Maat.

—The Scribe Nu

For more on the teachings of karma: Maat, Meskhenet, Djehuti, Shai and Rennenet see the books *The Book of the Dead, The 42 Precepts of Maat and The Philosophy of Righteous Action* by Dr. Muata Ashby.

---

[23] See bottom right

Appendix 1
Karma and Reincarnation

What is Ari?

The answer to this questions can be found in the *Ru Pert Em Heru* ⬭⎮⎮ ⎮ 𓆱 𓈖 ⋀ 𓅓 🔲 𓅿⎮ texts or "Book of Enlightenment" (also incorrectly known as the Book of the Dead, Book of Coming Forth by Day). The goddess 𓊵𓏏 ⬭⬭ 𓈖 𓂝 𓅓 *Meskhent* presides over the future birth of an individual but she represents only the culmination of the process, which has come to be known as ⎮ 𓂂 *Uhm-Ankh* "reincarnation" in modern times. In reality it is the individual who determines his or her own fate by the actions they perform in life. However, the wisdom of the ancient Egyptian Sages dictated that the process should be explained in mythological terms to help people better understand the philosophy. The process works as follows:

The deities *Shai* 𓍿𓋹 𓅓 𓏏𓏭 𓂝 𓈗 and ⭕ ⭕⭕ 𓅓 *Renunut* govern an individual's fate or destiny and their fortune. These deities are the hands of the great god Djehuti (he symbolizes the intellectual development of a human being) and he inscribes a person's fate once they have faced the scales of Maat, that is, they are judged in reference to their past ability to uphold Maat in life. A person's intellectual capacity reflects in their actions. Thus, it is fitting for the intellect to judge its own actions. Further, , God does not judge anyone because we are all essentially gods and goddesses, sparks of the same divinity, so God within us judges us. This is an objective judgment which only the individual is responsible for and it occurs at the unconscious level of the mind, beyond any interference from a persons personality or ego consciousness which is on the surface level of the mind; therefore, one's conscious desire to go to heaven at the time of death or one's conscious repentance at he time of death for misdeeds in life cannot overcome the weight of the ⬭ 𓈖 *ari* – (action thing done make something deed *Ari* -Karma) one has set up during a lifetime. So it is important to begin now to purify the heart and cleanse the soul so as to become 𓂝𓏏𓃀𓏏𓀁 **or** ⬭ *Maakheru* (true of speech-pure of heart) at the time of the judgment. The gods and goddesses are cosmic forces which only facilitate the process but from a mythological and philosophical standpoint they are concepts for understanding the mystical philosophy of the teaching.

Once the judgment has been rendered the goddess takes over and appoints the person's future family, place of birth, social status, etc. This is not meant as a punishment but as a process of leading the soul to the appropriate place where they can grow spiritually. If before you died you desired to be a musician the goddess will send you to a country, family and circumstances where this desire can be pursued. If you were a mugger in a past life you will end up in a place and situation where you will experience pain and suffering such as you caused to others and this experience will teach you to act otherwise in the future, thus improving your future birth. What you do after that is within the purview of your own free will and your actions in this new lifetime will engender and determine the next, and on and on. This process is 𓊵𓏏 ⬭⬭ 𓈖 𓂝𓏏 *Meskhent-* "destiny of birth." Meskhent is the manifestation of one's *shai-nefer* 𓍿𓋹 𓏏𓏭 𓄤 𓂝𓏏, positive destiny, or one's *shai-mit* 𓍿𓋹 𓅓 𓏏𓏭 𓂝 𓋲, negative destiny. This is ones harvest ⭕ ⭕⭕ 𓅓 or what one reaps from one's actions.

This is the process leading to *Uhm Ankh* (reincarnation). The objective is to lead oneself on a process of increasingly better births until it is possible to have spiritual inclination and the company of Sages and Saints who can lead a person to self-discovery

Introduction To MAAT PHILOSOPHY

(Rech-ab). When a person achieves this self-discovery they are referred to as Akh (the enlightened).

First, a person must become virtuous because this purifies the person's actions and thus, their Ari (karmic) basis. Negative Ari leads to negative situations but also to mental dullness and it is hard to understand the teachings when the mind is in a dull state, full of base thoughts, desires and feelings- this is the opposite of *Rech-ab*, it may be referred to as *inj-Set* (mind afflicted by fetters of Set). There is much mental agitation and suffering. The positive karmic basis allows harmonious surroundings and birth into the family of spiritually minded people as well as the company of Sages but most importantly the clarity of mind to understand the wisdom teachings. If the soul is judged to be pure in reference to Maat it will not be led to reincarnation Kemetic term (Uhem Ankh) but to the inner shrine where it meets its own higher self, i.e. God. Asar, the soul, meets Asar the Supreme Being. This meeting ends any future possibility of reincarnation. It means becoming one with the Divine Self. It is termed

Nehast (Resurrection), i.e. the Ausarian Resurrection. This is the only way to break the cycle of reincarnation.

So *ari* (karma) is not destiny but the accumulated unconscious impressions from desires, thoughts and feelings of the past (the present and previous lives) and not a set destiny. A person can change their *ari* by their present actions. The individual is always responsible for the present by the actions they performed previously which led them to the place they are today, etc. external factors can affect one's life but one is still in control ultimately of the response to those externalities of life (other people, circumstances, etc.). However, the present is not set. Otherwise people could not change and they would be destined to suffer or be happy based on some perverse cosmic joke. It is not like that. God has provided free will and with it a person can have a glorious life full of wisdom and prosperity or a life of strife, suffering and frustration based on egoism and egoistic desires and the actions one chooses.

The Ancient Egyptian word "Meskhent" is based on the word "*Mesken.*" *Mesken* means birthing place. Thus, *Meskhent* is the goddess (cosmic force) which presides over the *Mesken* of newborn souls. She makes effective, a persons desires and unconscious inclinations by placing a person who is to reincarnate into the appropriate circumstance for the new life based on previous actions and future potential.

HTP

Appendix 2

Ari and Ariu

What is Ariu? What we Neterians call 👁🐦 *ariu* (Indian -karma) and how does it operate in relation to a human being. *Ari* means deed, actions, etc. When a person performs any ari or deeds those deeds leave impressions in the mind, a form of residue. The memory of the action does not stay in the mind intact but the residue does. The residue is composed of a vague memory or thought related to the action; a feeling related to it, was it good or was it bad? And there is a small portion of life force energy associated with it. Ariu are the accumulated ari. If a sufficient number of ariu impressions are retained a person develops strong feelings towards the actions or objects associated with the actions. A person may repudiate some object or action or may love it without even recalling an exact memory of it. That residue is responsible and it can carry over from life to life. The feelings of the ariu can be powerful enough to impel a person towards a certain action, that is, to have a desire for something. The accumulated energy can become powerful enough to compel a person to do the action related to the desire. So controlling what impressions (ariu/residue) go into and become lodged in the unconscious mind is very important. The impure mind full of worldly ariu will lead a person to ignorant thoughts. Ariu remains dormant in the mind until stimulated by objects or actions in the external world or if strong enough they awaken via internal activation by the force of the desires. Until then they remain latent or inactive. That is the storehouse or content of a person's unconscious mind. So a person that may appear to be balanced, virtuous or pure may contain those ariu in the unconscious mind that still need to be purified. That person may achieve advancement in some areas but if the worldly ariu is not cleansed they may be pulled back down to worldly desires and activities. This has happened to many people. Some of the more popular examples are televangelists and preachers, or catholic priests who seem to be holy and pious and yet are later caught with prostitutes, molesting children, stealing church funds, etc. So it is important to follow the prescribed path under proper guidance to achieve true cleaning. Following the disciplines should be done under the guidance of a qualified spiritual preceptor so the aspirant may not go astray on the path of Maat.

As you know, the "Karmic Seeds" are actually impressions lodged in the unconscious mind which arise from a persons previous actions, thoughts, feelings, etc. As such they are infallible in their effect on the life of a human being because they sprout in the form of desires, which in turn lead to thoughts, and these in turn lead to more actions and those actions lead to more impressions, etc. and the cycle feeds on itself. As long as there is ignorance in the mind as to one's true nature (The Self). These impressions have control over the thoughts, actions and destiny of an un-enlightened human being. Even Jesus, Heru, Krishna, and Buddha could not escape this karmic law.

However, there is another rule of *ariu* that the yogis from ancient times discovered. With the dawning of self-knowledge, the karmic seeds, which would have sprouted as future thoughts and desires, become burnt up like popcorn. Popcorn cannot sprout any more and yet it can be eaten and enjoyed. An ordinary human being is constantly sewing seeds of karmic entanglement while a sage lives life like popped corn and at the end of his or her life the last kernel is popped and there are no more karmic seeds to propel future desires and the embodiments that would have come in the future. If this were not true, then there would be no escape from *ariu* and there would be no purpose to practice yoga, meditation or religion, etc.

The Path of Action and Enlightenment

Meditation eradictes *ariu* because it is like a light, which is turned on in a dark room. Think of a dark room full of junk. If the light is off you enter there and stumble. When the light is turned on you can see your way, avoid trouble and even clean the room out. Meditation is a light, which shines on the unconscious mind, illumining your true immortal self, which is the reality behind the desires, cravings and ignorance which is blocking your awareness of your own spirit. Impressions of fear, limitation, mortality, hatreds, pleasures, etc. are eradicated because they cannot exist in the light of your true nature, which transcends them. Therefore, *ariu* is burnt up like the popcorn. Your present embodiment continues and you exist as an ordinary human being but your mind does not produce or harbor illusions (Karmic seeds). You live out the rest of your life (popped pop corn) and do not produce new seeds and when you leave this earth you have nothing to hold you and you simply divest of your last drop of *ariu* (the body).

Therefore, Enlightenment is above and beyond *Ariu* and once enlightened the life of an enlightened person continues in accordance with his or her *ariu* but the soul and mind are no linger affected by whatever does or does not happen thereafter. Even a Sage may get sick or may have financial ups and downs or may experience many ordinary situations for the rest of his or her life due to previous *ariu*, but the practice of the teachings mitigates the negativity of those events and in any case enlightenment prevents suffering and there is no karmic entanglement.

Thus, in the state of ignorance, *ariu* and its fructification are infallible and there is no escape because this state is controlled by ignorance. Conversely, the yogic teachings, which lead to enlightenment, are also infallible in that they eradicate the cause of karmic fructification, i.e. ignorance of the self. This is why the practice of the Yogic disciplines is so important. God's Justice is not designed to produce suffering for every single mistake a person makes due to spiritual ignorance. God's compassion and mercy is embedded in the law of *ariu* . However, truth is more powerful than ignorance because truth has the virtue of being a reality while ignorance in an illusion. Thus, one instant of truth has the power to overcome centuries of ignorance. The dawning of enlightenment in the human mind sweeps away millions of years of ignorance and reincarnation and desires, etc. It is god's mercy and love which is transmitted to humanity through the work of sages and their students to spare people from the untold misery they would otherwise have to experience in the future. The wisdom of enlightenment through meditation dispels millions of years of ignorance just as a light can illumine a room even if it has been dark for millions of years. The light of self-knowledge is the truth, the power and the glory which dispels the ignorance of egoism and the illusions which a person is trapped in over countless reincarnations of the past.

HTP

Appendix 3

The Philosophy of Righteous Action, Social Order and Spiritual Upliftment of Humanity in Ancient Egypt and India

For any society, a philosophy of righteous action, which will promote social order and harmony, is essential to the creation of a civilized community and for the survival of the population as well as the prosperity of the country. This harmony and prosperity is the basis which allows higher spiritual study and practice to take place and for the culture to endure. A society wherein discontent and unrest distract people obstructs them from attaining the higher philosophy of self-discovery. The sages and saints of Ancient Kamit introduced and perfected this philosophy; they called it Maat. This teaching influenced the creation of the regulations for righteous conduct in Greek philosophy, Hinduism, Judaism, Chinese philosophy, Christianity and Islam, as all of these peoples had contact with Ancient Egypt.

Kamitan	Hindu-Buddhist	Jewish 10 Commandments	Chinese Confucianism And Taoism	Christian
Maat >5,000 B.C.E.	Dharma 800 B.C.E.	1,000 B.C.E.	500 B.C.E.	Beatitudes 0 B.C.E.

Maat represents the very order which constitutes creation, that is, Cosmic Order. Therefore, it is said that Ra, the Supreme Being, created the universe by putting Maat in the place of chaos. So creation itself is Maat. Creation without order is chaos. Maat is, therefore, a profound teaching in reference to the nature of creation and the manner in which human conduct should be cultivated. It contains a cosmic as well as worldly implication. It refers to a deep understanding of Divinity and the manner in which virtuous qualities can be developed in the human heart so as to come closer to the Divine.

Maat is a philosophy, a spiritual symbol as well as a cosmic energy or force which pervades the entire universe. Maat is personified by a goddess (divinity). She is the symbolic embodiment of world order, justice, righteousness, correctness, harmony and peace. She is also known by her headdress composed of a feather, which symbolizes the qualities just mentioned. She is a form of the Goddess Aset, who represents wisdom and spiritual awakening through balance and equanimity.

In Ancient Egypt, the judges and all those connected with the judicial system were initiated into the teachings of Maat (Judges were priests of Maat). Thus, those who would discharge the laws and regulations of society were well trained in the ethical and spiritual-mystical values of life. These principles included the application of justice and the responsibility to serve and promote harmony in society as well as the possibility for spiritual development in an atmosphere of freedom and peace, for only when there is justice and fairness in society can there be an abiding harmony and peace. Harmony and peace are necessary for the pursuit of true happiness and inner fulfillment in life. The opposite of *Maat* (righteousness) is *n-Maat* (unrighteousness) or *Isfet*.

Appendix 4
Maat and Themis

An important correlation can be found between the goddess of righteousness and justice, Maat, of Egypt and the goddess of divine justice, *Astraea* or *Themis,* of Greece.

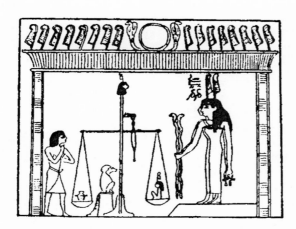 

Above left: The goddess Maat presiding over the balance scales of justice.
Above right: the goddess *Astraea* or *Themis* of Greece presiding over the balance scales of justice.

Appendix 5

Summary of Maat Philosophy

Maat Principles of Ethical Conduct	Maat Principles of Ethical Conduct
The Kamitan Path of Maat **42 Precepts and the Wisdom Texts[i]** • **Truth: Maat is Right Action-**Understanding the nature of the Divine, right from wrong as well as reality from unreality. • **Non-violence:** This is the philosophy of Imhotep, Akhnaton, Ptahotep and other Kamitan Sages, (approaching life in peace) and Ari-m-hetep (performing actions in peace and contentment. • **Right Action- self-control:** Living in accordance with the teachings of Maat. (integrity, honesty) • **Right Speech** speaking truth and refraining from angry speech. • **Right Worship:** Correct practice of religion including devotional practice, chanting, meditation, donating to the temple. • **Selfless Service:** Service to humanity includes taking care of the homeless, clotheless, the hungry and needy. • **Balance of Mind - Reason – Right Thinking:** Keeping the mind in balance so as not to lose the faculty of rational cognition. This involves a close attention (mindfulness) to control, prevent and eradicate the egoistic tendencies of the mind (arrogance, conceit, self-importance, greed, etc.). • **Not-stealing:** Stealing is a socially disruptive practice which denotes the degraded level of human consciousness and reinforces the ignorance of worldly desire and pleasure-seeking as well as greed. • **Sex-Sublimation:** Sexuality is one of the primal forces of nature which must be controlled in order to allow the personality to discover the higher perspectives of life. • **Maat Offering:** By acting with righteousness and attaining virtue the supreme offering is made through the Maat Offering in which the person making the offering enters into a meditative awareness through the ritual and sees {him/her} self as becoming one with Maat.	**Truth** (1), (6), (7), (9), (24) **Non-violence** (2), (3), (5), (12), (25), (26), (28), (30), (34) **Right Action- self-control (Living in accordance with the teachings of Maat)** (15), (20), (22), (36) **Right Speech** (11), (17), (23), (33), (35), (37) **Right Worship** (13), (21), (32), (38), (42) **Selfless Service** (29) **Balance of Mind - Reason – Right Thinking** (14), (16), (18), (31), (39) **Not-stealing** (4), (8), (10), (41) **Sex-Sublimation** (19), (27) The numbers within parenthesis represent the specific injunction in the 42 precepts of Maat that relate to the particular principle being expressed.

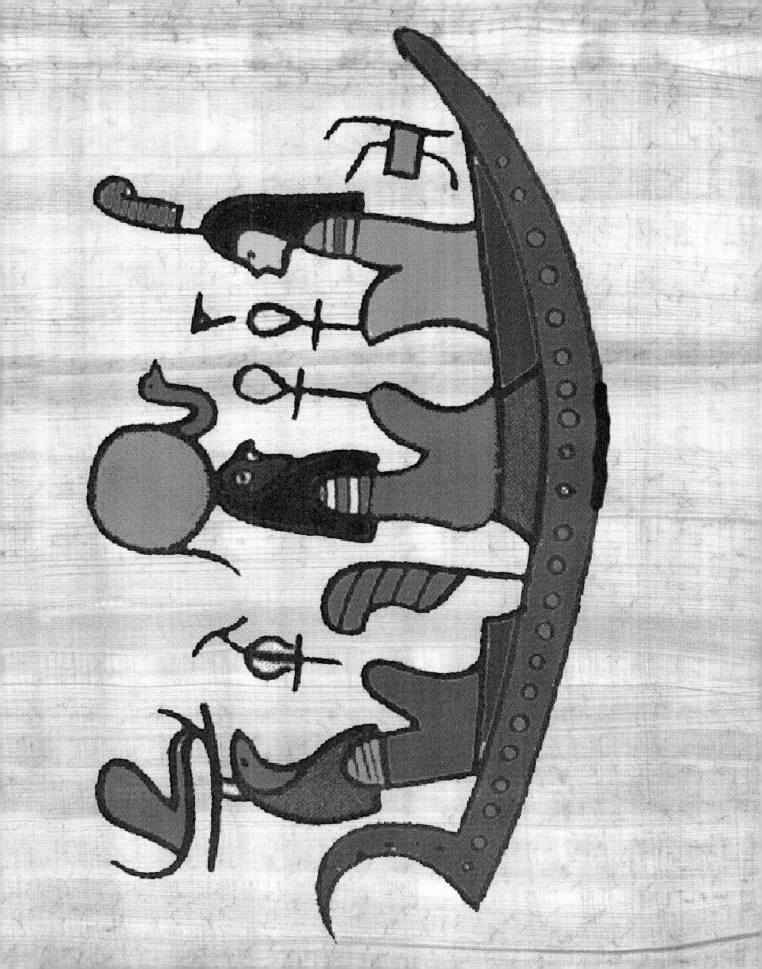

Questions for Reflection and Study

The following questions and exercises are designed for those taking the Egyptian Yoga course and are based on this volume and on Egyptian Yoga: The Philosophy of Enlightenment. However, anyone who works through them will gain a deeper insight into the themes expressed in this book.

1- Is nature a conglomeration of forces which are unpredictable and in need of control? Explain.
_____
_____
_____

2- What are the various injunctions of MAAT meant for?
_____
_____
_____

3- What is the basis upon which the Cosmic plan of Creation unfolds?
_____
_____
_____

4- Can anyone not perform actions?
_____
_____
_____

5- What guidelines have the ancient sages given?
_____
_____
_____

6- How can you become one with the Divine?
_____
_____
_____

The Path of Action and Enlightenment

7- How can you attain purity of heart?

_____

_____

_____

_____

8- What is behind every situation which presents itself to you?

_____

_____

_____

_____

9- What is everything a manifestation of?

_____

_____

_____

_____

10- Should you seek reward for your actions?

_____

_____

_____

11- What kind of work should you seek in life?

_____

_____

_____

_____

12- What happens when you perform jobs only for money or to fulfill an egoistic need?

_____

_____

_____

_____

13- How do people suffer in life due to their choices in occupation?

_____

_____

_____

_____

14- What is the principal issue of the Egyptian Book of Coming Forth By Day?

_____

_____

_____

15- Why is the name of the initiate changed to Asar in the Asarian mystery?

_____

_____
_____
_____
_____

16- What is your true name?

_____
_____
_____
_____

Exercise 1:

Remember the activities of the past week and identify any situations in which you acted selflessly. If you did not act selflessly visualize the situation as you would like it to happen next time. Relive the situation but this time using the teachings of Maat.

Exercise 2:

Examine your actions of the day. Look at yourself honestly and determine which actions you performed expecting to get something in return? Did you get what you expected? How did you feel?

Relive the situation but this time using the teachings of Maat. Perform the actions without seeking anything in return. Watch yourself as you become a witness to yourself and remain detached and inwardly fulfilled.

Exercise 3:

Examine your current occupation. How do you feel about it? Is it satisfying to your inner self? would you do it even if you were not paid to do it just because the doing allows you to feel fulfilled? or are you doing it based on greed or other egotistic feelings?

Rethink your decision to take this job. What would you really like to be doing? How can you use your inner talents to serve humanity and develop a true sense of peace and fulfillment within yourself?

If there is something else consider doing it on a part-time basis while continuing on your present job. See if there is a way to allow your inner self to express itself.

Visualize that occupation and see yourself becoming inwardly fulfilled. Feel that you are performing the occupation for the betterment of humanity in the name of the Divine Self. No one has to know, but the Divine Self, who is your innermost self.

Questions and Answers On Maat

Question

Greetings:

I would like some advice please. Actually I am in need of some advice. I have now been practicing the teachings to the best of my ability and understanding for about 17 months. Before I started practicing I was really laid back. I never let anyone see me get upset about anything and I showed very little emotion. In fact I did not think that anything really bothered me at all. At the time I thought that I was a person who did not let things bother me. I thought that people who could not control their emotions were weak, and I thought that things really had no affect on me.

Since I have been practicing the teachings, while I have attempted to control my thoughts and actions, and master my emotions, the exact opposite has happened. I have begun to take things personally, people get on my nerves, (especially my family) I blow up and get angry quickly and it seems like I am becoming the person who I did not like previously. Even after meditation it seems like it takes very little to set me off. This happens about once a week and I wind having a foul disposition. This disposition lasts 2-4 days sometimes. I don't stop my Sheti but I do sometimes forget to practice control. My wife has even commented that ever since I have been studying I have become more "sensitive" to things and irritable, which makes me get upset which was not the case previously.

I don't get it. It is my understanding that progress in the teaching is measured in one's ability to detach from the world and not be affected by it. It seems like I am becoming more affected by it. The only thing I can think of is that my practice and understanding of the teaching must be off because the opposite is happening to me.

Any advice. I do the breathing exercises, prayer, chanting, Tief Neteru exercises and Meditate in the mornings and do the same except for the exercises 3-4 times a week during the evenings.

Hetep

Answer

Greetings,

Take heart, what you are describing is a natural stage on the spiritual path. Actually it is a sign that you are practicing the teachings and indeed making progress. How is this possible? Consider that when a person turns to a healthy vegetarian diet after consuming meat there is a cleansing reaction. The good food causes a cleansing effect and the person appears to get sick from the good food. In reality a cleansing process is going on because the good food is pushing out the poisons ingested previously. That person may have appeared to be healthy but internally there were many toxins. This is the detoxification process. For the Ka and Ba (mind and soul) there is also a cleaning that must occur. You are now only learning that your idea of being more advanced and of having mastered some lower levels was a misconception, an illusion. It is good for you to realize this. And yes you will become more sensitive and since you are in a householder environment your challenge is more difficult than someone living alone in a temple. Family relations are more intense because the involvement with family members is very complex. Nevertheless, as you continue to practice the teaching these complexes will be resolved and transcended. Yet consider that your progress will be faster than the person living alone because your failings will be exposed more efficiently and you no longer have the illusions about the world to fall back on that most people have (since you are a follower of the teaching). You cannot just "kiss and make up" because you know the illusoriness of life. Further, realize that 17 months is a short time and hearing the teaching and interacting with the teacher is more powerful than reading books alone or practicing the teaching on your own. Books and self-taught practices are prone to error and you may be experiencing the strong effect of attending classes which you were not exposed to before. What you are going through is called "personality integration." It is the necessary process whereby you are challenged, then you must reflect and come to terms with your experiences. Do not wonder why, simply rest assured that it is necessary and that the outcome will be for your ultimate benefit. The Divine Self has made things this way for a reason, have faith. However, do not keep yourself in a pressure cooker all the time, relax from the teachings as it were. Take your family to a positive movie, eat with them (vegetarian food). Show them you care but internally work to care with the higher vision. Take breaks also by going on retreats so that you may reflect and meditate on the teaching. Constant pressure is not necessary or advised to promote enlightenment. It often leads to an imbalanced personality and this is counterproductive, causing strife, anger etc., especially because the feeling comes in that you have failed in attaining the level you thought you were at, etc. Leave these thoughts behind.

Yet there needs to be a balance in life even for the advanced aspirants. Seek this balance by having faith and trust in these words. Next accept the negative that seems to be coming forth from the deeper levels of the personality and allow it to be cleansed. Do not own it but simply marvel at the complexes and thank goddess *Maat* for assisting you to see them because they would have been obstacles to enlightenment had they remained hidden. Even when an episode of anger or irritability occurs, remember these words and they will help you to return to calm. If need be remove yourself from the situation until you are calm and then return. Go to your meditation area, utter some chants, read some of the text or read this letter again and again and you will find solace and peace. Realize that the negative actions are born of the egoistic impressions of the mind due to previous ignorance. Offer those actions to the Divine just as you should offer the positive actions as well. Try to follow *Maat* but do not own the outcomes of your actions or their consequences. Let the goddess handle those. You work to purify yourself and the rest will come together in time. Continue the daily disciplines and judge your progress by how fast you return to normalcy and balance; how fast you return to self-control. If the negative disposition now lasts 2-4 days sometimes see if it goes to 1-3 days to 1 day to ½ day to hours and even minutes. This is mastery of the emotions. In this mastery they are controlled, made slaves and are no longer masters over you, controlling your personality making you angry against your will, etc.

The Path of Action and Enlightenment

Soon you will develop deeper sensitivity and you will know when anger is entering the mind and you will be able to stop it there before it comes to the surface and if you can control it before it expresses you will have a better chance to overcome it and the trouble that its consequences produce in your environment. In any case, seek to follow *Maat*. *Maat* says, "I have not allowed myself to become angry without cause." Sometimes there is just cause for anger and sometimes it is necessary even for sages to show anger. If a child is in some imminent danger it is appropriate to angrily stop her from injuring herself or if some injustice is done it may be appropriate to show anger to convey the emotional content needed to reach the person perpetrating the injustice. But in sages these emotions are controlled and harnessed. Sages do not really become angry or hate anything internally even if they appear to be. The emotions do not control the sages. Examine the cause of your anger. If it is justified (needed to achieve a goal) show it to the extent it assists to get the point across. If it is not justified proceed as outlined above. Remember that to reach the sagehood level the sages had to practice control as you are today. The fire of worldly situations is the forge that molds sages but in order for this process to work there must be a blacksmith to shape the aspirant, this is the teacher. The soul is the iron to be shaped, the teaching is the anvil upon which the soul is worked by the sage and the fire of life are the worldly situations. However, if the fire is too hot the metal melts away. If it is too cold there is no way to bend the metal. The metal cannot shape itself on its own by studying books or imagining things. So there must be challenge and stress but this is to be managed in doses and not constant. The teacher must help the student to apply the right amount of pressure, striking with the hammer at the right times and placing the iron in the fire or water at the right times. An aspirant must learn to relax and accept the imperfections of the personality even while working towards perfection in a balanced manner. This is the path of Ari m Hetep (Yoga of right actions). You can see how magnanimous and advanced this philosophy is and how its deeper insights cannot come from reading books on *Maat* or simplistic ideals such as do good and bee good or be balanced. Aspirants grow when they go through the process of life, being led by the authentic teacher and an authentic teaching.

HTP – Peace and blessings

Sebai Maa (Dr. Muata Ashby)

MAAT PHILOSOPHY & The Wisdom of Maati

Question

Sebai Dr. Muata Ashby,

I have purchased the Home Study Guide booklet, because I want to tap into the wisdom of my ancestors--the builders of the greatest civilization ever known.

I am particularly interested in making *MAAT* the emphasis of my spiritual studies. I have already read Egyptian Yoga 1 & 2, and Egyptian Proverbs.

As a full time worker and part-time college student, I must be efficient in how I use my time; thus I want to be systematic in my study of the wisdom teachings. On pages 19-20 of the study guide, the class sequence places *Maat* fifth in an eight step process. However, on page ten, spiritual aspirants like myself are told to study *Maat* "If you are interested in the path of righteous action".

 In which direction should I go to begin my studies?

Answer

Greetings, the Home Study Guide booklet contains a general program of study for those who do not have a particular interest or who are new to the teaching. If you have a specific affinity with a particular aspect of the teaching such as *Maat* Philosophy then that should be the basis or foundation of your studies. Therefore, you should concentrate on the books that discuss the *Maat* path: Wisdom of *Maat*i, The 42 Precepts of *Maat* and the Wisdom Texts, The Book of the Dead. Also there are audio series that should be listened to and also videos. If you are further interested you should attend the internet classes and also the upcoming seminar.

May the goddess *Maat* bless you with all Righteousness.

HTP-Peace

𓊪𓂝𓏤𓈖𓏏𓄿 𓅃𓅃𓅃
Sebai Maa (Dr. Muata Ashby)

The Path of Action and Enlightenment

Greetings Seba Maa:

Query? If creation really doesn't exist, fear itself must be an illusion. My ultimate fear is death but I also fear getting hurt. I think I understand that creation only exists in the mind, however this understanding is not helping me transcend my fear of death. Is there any technique that will allow one to work on this aspect of one's personality to eradicate it? This seems like a tough to cookie to crack but I want to tackle it head-on.
Any advice?

Hetep

Greetings,

The teaching is not that Creation does not exist but rather that its existence is misconceived by the ignorant mind. Indeed, overcoming death is the last obstacle to attaining spiritual enlightenment and immortality. Fear is therefore, a psychological obstacle created by the illusion of life. That is a person perceives they are "living" because they are awake and breathing but yet what can be said about a person who has drowned in an accident or been buried alive and the heart has stopped and there are no brain waves and then they are revived? To overcome death you must understand what life really is and this is what the Prt m Hru text is all about; it is the book of life. The more you cling to the mortal life and the idea that you are an individual with a body and senses and flesh and blood you will be more fearful of losing that life because this is all you know. And conversely the more you realize you transcend the limited and finite body and the world of time and space the more fearless you become and the more exhilarating life becomes. This is all just philosophy; what is needed is for you to put this into practice to make it effective.

First, be steady with the daily spiritual disciplines, next study the teaching closely and next take time to reflect upon it and then meditate upon it in silence. Apply the teaching of *Maat* to your day to day life and bring order and stability to your life. Resolve to relinquish fear and insecurity and embrace spirit and peace even if it is not forthcoming right away. Bring yourself to balance so that you may practice profound meditation the kind which will allow you to discover the truth behind the teachings first hand instead of just theoretically that you are immortal and eternal. Resolve to throw off the illusion that you are limited and feeble and accept the mantle of golden feathers that is bestowed upon those who follow in the footsteps of Heru, the Golden Glorious spirit within. Repeatedly uplift the mind with the truths of the teaching and counteract the ignorant thoughts each time they emerge. Work to prevent the negative thinking by becoming a keen observer of the mind in a detached fashion. Resolve to leave behind worldly desires and pursue the desire for self-discovery and enlightenment (Nehast). Then you will move away from fear, sorrow, ignorance and delusion. Then you will discover incomparable peace, boundless joy and freedom from fear and ignorance once and for all.

HTP-Peace

Sebai Maa (Dr. Muata Ashby)

MAAT PHILOSOPHY & The Wisdom of Maati

Udja Sebai Maa

The *Maat* Cosmic Principle articulates: Do no violence (to any one or anything); and the virtue & diet; of Ari (Karma) articulates: law of cause and effect- a cosmic principle! What you do comes back to you! In other words: "If you kill what you eat, what you eat will kill you.

Question:

Considering the above statements are true and it is, what about vegetables, plants and the accidental killing of microscopic insects life by way of the washing of the hands and body. Aren't these living organism or life also? How do they fit in to the above proverbs or teachings?

Thank you

Answer

In fact from a relative perspective there is no way to escape violence of some kind or other in life as killing and creating is part of Creation as you have stated, in killing microbes, consuming vegetables, etc. What the teaching refers to is malice of forethought, and egoistic involvement in violence. Killing something or someone by accident does not count. Violence as it is performed by the universe is merely an egoistic judgment by a human being, for what destroys actually also creates. So Goddess creates and destroys for the greater purpose of existence and that is without malice or preference. So from her perspective she neither destroys nor creates but establishes order, balance and harmony. What is prohibited therefore is actions with malice, that is egoistic actions of passion or desire. If you kill with passion, anger, hatred, greed, etc it is evil; furthermore it is futile, for it will not lead to the desired outcome (happiness-attaining one's desire). killing out of necessity to survive (not preemptively) is not killing but following the law of *Maat* actually, for it is righteous that life is to be preserved and order and balance and truth protected. in the hierarchy of life lower sentient forms have less priority than the higher and so are accorded less prominence especially when overstepping their boundaries. For example, microbes live in the body, but if they overrun the body they will cause disease; they are violating the *Maat*ian order and must be controlled and brought to their balance. Taking vitamins, herbs, etc, kills some of them to bring them back to order. A few roaches can live in a house with people but if too many abound then it is a person's right, nay, even a duty to kill them off before they cause disease; to restore order and balance. Philosophically (which is the only important aspect for aspirants to consider) Killing vegetables is not violence because it is the process for human survival established by *Maat* (through Neteru (nature)). Ignorant human beings believing they are creating or killing is a violation of *Maat* for only she established that order. Such a belief is based on spiritual ignorance that gives rise to ego and egoism. This is the first error. If a human being takes on the burden of thinking they are killing or creating they are assuming the responsibility and consequences of those beliefs and will suffer accordingly (while creating (making a baby, building an object, making music, painting a picture, etc.) seems to be a joyous process but actually if done egoistically it is a precursor for pain and suffering). Only god creates

The Path of Action and Enlightenment

through you, you do nothing and so should not take on the egoistic burden. God has done it so let God bear the consequence. Killing animals is violence because human beings do not need to kill them to survive and indeed all evidence shows that it is detrimental to the human body to eat animals. It is done for the sake of egoistic pleasure- one of the highest sins of human existence. This is why an aspirant must learn to adopt and implement the *Maat* philosophy, to live by truth and not egoistic notions, to act with peace, neutrality, based on truth and not egoistic desire, for that is the way to hell and reincarnation. The path of *Maat* is the way of peace and freedom and immortality. When an aspirant has reached perfection in action there will be peace and harmony and balance no matter if there is killing going on or if there is creating and then such a one has become one with the goddess and in so doing has attained Maakheru, the ultimate truth; one has transcended the relative perspective, the lower existence in time and space. For them there is no death, no birth; they have transcended the opposites of Creation and cease to exist in the past or future but have attained the eternal present. Glory be to *Maat*! Isn't she just wonderful?

HTP

Sebai Maa (Dr. Muata Ashby)

Question

Udja,

I have a question.

I would like to find out what is the best way to protect oneself from attacks from others such as spells.

What did the ancient Kamites do to protect themselves from sorcery?

htp

Answer

Udja,

The best defense against psychic attack (negative influences from evil spirits, demons etc.) and evil eye (negative thoughts) from others is to become purified by _Maat_. That is to study the philosophy and then follow the discipline of _Maat_. Discover the deep meaning of truth, righteousness and nonviolence. Reinforce this practice the scriptures, Chants and songs of _Maat_ and with ritual purification and daily worship (carry out the daily worship program - daily-without fail). Practice non-violence- do not return evil thoughts to the evil minded- that brings you down to the level of demoniac consciousness with them. Rather, forgive them and tend to your own spiritual practice and keep Shedy- meet and associate as much as possible with those who are like you practicing the philosophy of _Maat_ and others who practice _Maat_ in different forms (those who are righteous, have integrity and non-violence. Righteousness, purity of heart, body-mind and soul is like a suit of armor against inimical forces of all kinds and also the doorway that opens up the inner peace needed to discover the inner reaches of the Divine Self. Goddess _Maat_ will herself protect you from inimical forces. Then you will repel those negative sentiments and thoughts and you will be free to pursue the true meaning of life. Resources: read the book _Introduction to Maat Philosophy_ and study the lecture series _42 Precepts of Maat and the Philosophy of Righteous Action._

HTP
Peace be with you

𓏤𓇳𓈏𓏭𓅆𓃀𓃀𓃀

Sebai Maa (Dr. Muata Ashby)

Doing Maat is breath to the nose.

I am pure. I am pure. I am Pure.
I have washed my front parts with the waters of libations, I have cleansed my hinder parts
with drugs which make wholly clean, and my inward parts have been washed in the liquor
of Maat.
-The Scribe Nu

MAAT
Be True

INDEX

The Path of Action and Enlightenment

Other Books From C M Books

P.O.Box 570459
Miami, Florida, 33257
(305) 378-6253 Fax: (305) 378-6253

This book is part of a series on the study and practice of Ancient Egyptian Yoga and Mystical Spirituality based on the writings of Dr. Muata Abhaya Ashby. They are also part of the Egyptian Yoga Course provided by the Sema Institute of Yoga. Below you will find a listing of the other books in this series. For more information send for the Egyptian Yoga Book-Audio-Video Catalog or the Egyptian Yoga Course Catalog.

Now you can study the teachings of Egyptian and Indian Yoga wisdom and Spirituality with the Egyptian Yoga Mystical Spirituality Series. The Egyptian Yoga Series takes you through the Initiation process and lead you to understand the mysteries of the soul and the Divine and to attain the highest goal of life: ENLIGHTENMENT. The *Egyptian Yoga Series*, takes you on an in depth study of Ancient Egyptian mythology and their inner mystical meaning. Each Book is prepared for the serious student of the mystical sciences and provides a study of the teachings along with exercises, assignments and projects to make the teachings understood and effective in real life. The Series is part of the Egyptian Yoga course but may be purchased even if you are not taking the course. The series is ideal for study groups.

Prices subject to change.

MAAT PHILOSOPHY & The Wisdom of Maati

1. EGYPTIAN YOGA: THE PHILOSOPHY OF ENLIGHTENMENT An original, fully illustrated work, including hieroglyphs, detailing the meaning of the Egyptian mysteries, tantric yoga, psycho-spiritual and physical exercises. Egyptian Yoga is a guide to the practice of the highest spiritual philosophy which leads to absolute freedom from human misery and to immortality. It is well known by scholars that Egyptian philosophy is the basis of Western and Middle Eastern religious philosophies such as *Christianity, Islam, Judaism,* the *Kabala*, and Greek philosophy, but what about Indian philosophy, Yoga and Taoism? What were the original teachings? How can they be practiced today? What is the source of pain and suffering in the world and what is the solution? Discover the deepest mysteries of the mind and universe within and outside of your self. 8.5" X 11" ISBN: 1-884564-01-1 Soft $19.95

2. EGYPTIAN YOGA II: The Supreme Wisdom of Enlightenment by Dr. Muata Ashby ISBN 1-884564-39-9 $23.95 U.S. In this long awaited sequel to *Egyptian Yoga: The Philosophy of Enlightenment* you will take a fascinating and enlightening journey back in time and discover the teachings which constituted the epitome of Ancient Egyptian spiritual wisdom. What are the disciplines which lead to the fulfillment of all desires? Delve into the three states of consciousness (waking, dream and deep sleep) and the fourth state which transcends them all, Neberdjer, "The Absolute." These teachings of the city of Waset (Thebes) were the crowning achievement of the Sages of Ancient Egypt. They establish the standard mystical keys for understanding the profound mystical symbolism of the Triad of human consciousness.

3. THE KEMETIC DIET: GUIDE TO HEALTH, DIET AND FASTING Health issues have always been important to human beings since the beginning of time. The earliest records of history show that the art of healing was held in high esteem since the time of Ancient Egypt. In the early 20th century, medical doctors had almost attained the status of sainthood by the promotion of the idea that they alone were "scientists" while other healing modalities and traditional healers who did not follow the "scientific method' were nothing but superstitious, ignorant charlatans who at best would take the money of their clients and at worst kill them with the unscientific "snake oils" and "irrational theories". In the late 20th century, the failure of the modern medical establishment's ability to lead the general public to good health, promoted the move by many in society towards "alternative medicine". Alternative medicine disciplines are those healing modalities which do not adhere to the philosophy of allopathic medicine. Allopathic medicine is what medical doctors practice by an large. It is the theory that disease is caused by agencies outside the body such as bacteria, viruses or physical means which affect the body. These can therefore be treated by medicines and therapies The natural healing method began in the absence of extensive technologies with the idea that all the answers for health may be found in nature or rather, the deviation from nature. Therefore, the health of the body can be restored by correcting the aberration and thereby restoring balance. This is the area that will be covered in this volume. Allopathic techniques have their place in the art of healing. However, we should not forget that the body is a grand achievement of the spirit and built into it is the capacity to maintain itself and heal itself. Ashby, Muata ISBN: 1-884564-49-6 $28.95

4. INITIATION INTO EGYPTIAN YOGA Shedy: Spiritual discipline or program, to go deeply into the mysteries, to study the mystery teachings and literature profoundly, to penetrate the mysteries. You will learn about the mysteries of initiation into the teachings and practice of Yoga and how to become an Initiate of the mystical sciences. This insightful manual is the first in a series which introduces you to the goals of daily spiritual and yoga practices: Meditation, Diet, Words of Power and the ancient wisdom teachings. 8.5" X 11" ISBN 1-884564-02-X Soft Cover $24.95 U.S.

5. *THE AFRICAN ORIGINS OF CIVILIZATION, MYSTICAL RELIGION AND YOGA PHILOSOPHY* HARD COVER EDITION ISBN: 1-884564-50-X $80.00 U.S.   81/2" X 11"   Part 1, Part 2, Part 3 in one volume 683 Pages Hard Cover First Edition Three volumes in one. Over the past several years I have been asked to put together in one volume the most important evidences showing the correlations and common teachings between Kamitan (Ancient Egyptian) culture and religion and that of India. The questions of the history of Ancient Egypt, and the latest archeological evidences showing civilization and culture in Ancient Egypt and its spread to other countries, has intrigued many scholars as well as mystics over the years. Also, the possibility that Ancient Egyptian Priests and Priestesses migrated to Greece, India and other countries to carry on the traditions of the Ancient Egyptian Mysteries, has been speculated over the years as well. In chapter 1 of the book *Egyptian Yoga The Philosophy of Enlightenment,* 1995, I first introduced the deepest

The Path of Action and Enlightenment

comparison between Ancient Egypt and India that had been brought forth up to that time. Now, in the year 2001 this new book, *THE AFRICAN ORIGINS OF CIVILIZATION, MYSTICAL RELIGION AND YOGA PHILOSOPHY,* more fully explores the motifs, symbols and philosophical correlations between Ancient Egyptian and Indian mysticism and clearly shows not only that Ancient Egypt and India were connected culturally but also spiritually. How does this knowledge help the spiritual aspirant? This discovery has great importance for the Yogis and mystics who follow the philosophy of Ancient Egypt and the mysticism of India. It means that India has a longer history and heritage than was previously understood. It shows that the mysteries of Ancient Egypt were essentially a yoga tradition which did not die but rather developed into the modern day systems of Yoga technology of India. It further shows that African culture developed Yoga Mysticism earlier than any other civilization in history. All of this expands our understanding of the unity of culture and the deep legacy of Yoga, which stretches into the distant past, beyond the Indus Valley civilization, the earliest known high culture in India as well as the Vedic tradition of Aryan culture. Therefore, Yoga culture and mysticism is the oldest known tradition of spiritual development and Indian mysticism is an extension of the Ancient Egyptian mysticism. By understanding the legacy which Ancient Egypt gave to India the mysticism of India is better understood and by comprehending the heritage of Indian Yoga, which is rooted in Ancient Egypt the Mysticism of Ancient Egypt is also better understood. This expanded understanding allows us to prove the underlying kinship of humanity, through the common symbols, motifs and philosophies which are not disparate and confusing teachings but in reality expressions of the same study of truth through metaphysics and mystical realization of Self. (HARD COVER)

6. AFRICAN ORIGINS BOOK 1 PART 1 African Origins of African Civilization, Religion, Yoga Mysticism and Ethics Philosophy-Soft Cover $24.95 ISBN: 1-884564-55-0

7. AFRICAN ORIGINS BOOK 2 PART 2 African Origins of Western Civilization, Religion and Philosophy(Soft) -Soft Cover $24.95 ISBN: 1-884564-56-9

8. EGYPT AND INDIA (AFRICAN ORIGINS BOOK 3 PART 3) African Origins of Eastern Civilization, Religion, Yoga Mysticism and Philosophy-Soft Cover $29.95 (Soft) ISBN: 1-884564-57-7

9. THE MYSTERIES OF ISIS: The Path of Wisdom, Immortality and Enlightenment   Through the study of ancient myth and the illumination of initiatic understanding the idea of God is expanded from the mythological comprehension to the metaphysical. Then this metaphysical understanding is related to you, the student, so as to begin understanding your true divine nature. ISBN 1-884564-24-0 $24.99

10. EGYPTIAN PROVERBS: TEMT TCHAAS *Temt Tchaas* means: collection of ——Ancient Egyptian Proverbs How to live according to MAAT Philosophy. Beginning Meditation. All proverbs are indexed for easy searches. For the first time in one volume, ——Ancient Egyptian Proverbs, wisdom teachings and meditations, fully illustrated with hieroglyphic text and symbols. EGYPTIAN PROVERBS is a unique collection of knowledge and wisdom which you can put into practice today and transform your life. 5.5"x 8.5" $14.95 U.S   ISBN: 1-884564-00-3

11. THE PATH OF DIVINE LOVE The Process of Mystical Transformation and The Path of Divine Love This Volume will focus on the ancient wisdom teachings and how to use them in a scientific process for self-transformation. Also, this volume will detail the process of transformation from ordinary consciousness to cosmic consciousness through the integrated practice of the teachings and the path of Devotional Love toward the Divine. 5.5"x 8.5" ISBN 1-884564-11-9 $22.99

12. INTRODUCTION TO MAAT PHILOSOPHY: Spiritual Enlightenment Through the Path of Virtue Known as Karma Yoga in India, the teachings of MAAT for living virtuously and with orderly wisdom are explained and the student is to begin practicing the precepts of Maat in daily life so as to promote the process of purification of the heart in preparation for the judgment of the soul. This judgment will be understood not as an event that will occur at the time of death but as an event that occurs continuously, at every moment in the life of the individual. The student will learn how to become allied with the forces of the Higher Self and to thereby begin cleansing the mind (heart) of impurities so as to attain a higher vision of reality. ISBN 1-884564-20-8 $22.99

13.   MEDITATION The Ancient Egyptian Path to Enlightenment   Many people do not know about the rich history of meditation practice in Ancient Egypt. This volume outlines the theory of meditation and presents the Ancient Egyptian Hieroglyphic text which give instruction as to the nature of the mind and its three modes of expression. It also presents the texts which give instruction on the practice of meditation for spiritual Enlightenment and unity with the Divine. This volume allows the reader to begin practicing meditation by explaining, in easy to understand terms, the simplest form of meditation and working up to the most advanced form which was practiced in ancient times and which is still practiced by yogis around the world in modern times. ISBN 1-884564-27-7 $24.99

14.   THE GLORIOUS LIGHT MEDITATION TECHNIQUE OF ANCIENT EGYPT ISBN: 1-884564-15-1$14.95 (PB) New for the year 2000. This volume is based on the earliest known instruction in history given for the practice of formal meditation. Discovered by Dr. Muata Ashby, it is inscribed on the walls of the Tomb of Seti I in Thebes Egypt. This volume details the philosophy and practice of this unique system of meditation originated in Ancient Egypt and the earliest practice of meditation known in the world which occurred in the most advanced African Culture.

15.   THE SERPENT POWER: The Ancient Egyptian Mystical Wisdom of the Inner Life Force.   This Volume specifically deals with the latent life Force energy of the universe and in the human body, its control and sublimation. How to develop the Life Force energy of the subtle body. This Volume will introduce the esoteric wisdom of the science of how virtuous living acts in a subtle and mysterious way to cleanse the latent psychic energy conduits and vortices of the spiritual body. ISBN 1-884564-19-4 $22.95

16.   EGYPTIAN YOGA MEDITATION IN MOTION Thef Neteru: *The Movement of The Gods and Goddesses* Discover the physical postures and exercises practiced thousands of years ago in Ancient Egypt which are today known as Yoga exercises. This work is based on the pictures and teachings from the Creation story of Ra, The Asarian Resurrection Myth and the carvings and reliefs from various Temples in Ancient Egypt 8.5" X 11" ISBN 1-884564-10-0 Soft Cover $18.99   Exercise video $21.99

17.   EGYPTIAN TANTRA YOGA: The Art of Sex Sublimation and Universal Consciousness This Volume will expand on the male and female principles within the human body and in the universe and further detail the sublimation of sexual energy into spiritual energy. The student will study the deities Min and Hathor, Asar and Aset, Geb and Nut and discover the mystical implications for a practical spiritual discipline. This Volume will also focus on the Tantric aspects of Ancient Egyptian and Indian mysticism, the purpose of sex and the mystical teachings of sexual sublimation which lead to self-knowledge and Enlightenment. 5.5"x 8.5" ISBN 1-884564-03-8 $24.95

18.   ASARIAN RELIGION: RESURRECTING OSIRIS The path of Mystical Awakening and the Keys to Immortality NEW REVISED AND EXPANDED EDITION! The Ancient Sages created stories based on human and superhuman beings whose struggles, aspirations, needs and desires ultimately lead them to discover their true Self. The myth of Aset, Asar and Heru is no exception in this area. While there is no one source where the entire story may be found, pieces of it are inscribed in various ancient Temples walls, tombs, steles and papyri. For the first time available, the complete myth of Asar, Aset and Heru has been compiled from original Ancient Egyptian, Greek and Coptic Texts. This epic myth has been richly illustrated with reliefs from the Temple of Heru at Edfu, the Temple of Aset at Philae, the Temple of Asar at Abydos, the Temple of Hathor at Denderah and various papyri, inscriptions and reliefs. Discover the myth which inspired the teachings of the *Shetaut Neter* (Egyptian Mystery System - Egyptian Yoga) and the Egyptian Book of Coming Forth By Day. Also, discover the three levels of Ancient Egyptian Religion, how to understand the mysteries of the Duat or Astral World and how to discover the abode of the Supreme in the Amenta, *The Other World*   The ancient religion of Asar, Aset and Heru, if properly understood, contains all of the elements necessary to lead the sincere aspirant to attain immortality through inner self-discovery. This volume presents the entire myth and explores the main mystical themes and rituals associated with the myth for understating human existence, creation and the way to achieve spiritual emancipation - *Resurrection.* The Asarian myth is so powerful that it influenced and is still having an effect on the major world religions. Discover the origins and mystical meaning of the Christian Trinity, the

The Path of Action and Enlightenment

Eucharist ritual and the ancient origin of the birthday of Jesus Christ. Soft Cover ISBN: 1-884564-27-5 $24.95

19. THE EGYPTIAN BOOK OF THE DEAD MYSTICISM OF THE PERT EM HERU $26.95   ISBN# 1-884564-28-3 Size: 8½" X 11" I Know myself, I know myself, I am One With God!–From the Pert Em Heru "The Ru Pert em Heru" or "Ancient Egyptian Book of The Dead," or "Book of Coming Forth By Day" as it is more popularly known, has fascinated the world since the successful translation of Ancient Egyptian hieroglyphic scripture over 150 years ago. The astonishing writings in it reveal that the Ancient Egyptians believed in life after death and in an ultimate destiny to discover the Divine. The elegance and aesthetic beauty of the hieroglyphic text itself has inspired many see it as an art form in and of itself. But is there more to it than that? Did the Ancient Egyptian wisdom contain more than just aphorisms and hopes of eternal life beyond death? In this volume Dr. Muata Ashby, the author of over 25 books on Ancient Egyptian Yoga Philosophy has produced a new translation of the original texts which uncovers a mystical teaching underlying the sayings and rituals instituted by the Ancient Egyptian Sages and Saints. "Once the philosophy of Ancient Egypt is understood as a mystical tradition instead of as a religion or primitive mythology, it reveals its secrets which if practiced today will lead anyone to discover the glory of spiritual self-discovery. The Pert em Heru is in every way comparable to the Indian Upanishads or the Tibetan Book of the Dead." - Muata Abhaya Ashby

20. ANUNIAN THEOLOGY THE MYSTERIES OF RA The Philosophy of Anu and The Mystical Teachings of The Ancient Egyptian Creation Myth Discover the mystical teachings contained in the Creation Myth and the gods and goddesses who brought creation and human beings into existence. The Creation Myth holds the key to understanding the universe and for attaining spiritual Enlightenment. ISBN: 1-884564-38-0 40 pages $14.95

21. MYSTERIES OF MIND AND MEMPHITE THEOLOGY Mysticism of Ptah, Egyptian Physics and Yoga Metaphysics and the Hidden properties of Matter   This Volume will go deeper into the philosophy of God as creation and will explore the concepts of modern science and how they correlate with ancient teachings. This Volume will lay the ground work for the understanding of the philosophy of universal consciousness and the initiatic/yogic insight into who or what is God? ISBN 1-884564-07-0 $21.95

22. THE GODDESS AND THE EGYPTIAN MYSTERIESTHE PATH OF THE GODDESS THE GODDESS PATH The Secret Forms of the Goddess and the Rituals of Resurrection The Supreme Being may be worshipped as father or as mother. *Ushet Rekhat* or *Mother Worship*, is the spiritual process of worshipping the Divine in the form of the Divine Goddess. It celebrates the most important forms of the Goddess including *Nathor, Maat, Aset, Arat, Amentet and Hathor* and explores their mystical meaning as well as the rising of *Sirius,* the star of Aset (Aset) and the new birth of Hor (Heru). The end of the year is a time of reckoning, reflection and engendering a new or renewed positive movement toward attaining spiritual Enlightenment. The Mother Worship devotional meditation ritual, performed on five days during the month of December and on New Year's Eve, is based on the Ushet Rekhit. During the ceremony, the cosmic forces, symbolized by Sirius - and the constellation of Orion ---, are harnessed through the understanding and devotional attitude of the participant. This propitiation draws the light of wisdom and health to all those who share in the ritual, leading to prosperity and wisdom. $14.95 ISBN 1-884564-18-6

23. *THE MYSTICAL JOURNEY FROM JESUS TO CHRIST* $24.95   ISBN# 1-884564-05-4 size: 8½" X 11" Discover the ancient Egyptian origins of Christianity before the Catholic Church and learn the mystical teachings given by Jesus to assist all humanity in becoming Christlike. Discover the secret meaning of the Gospels that were discovered in Egypt. Also discover how and why so many Christian churches came into being. Discover that the Bible still holds the keys to mystical realization even though its original writings were changed by the church. Discover how to practice the original teachings of Christianity which leads to the Kingdom of Heaven.

24. THE STORY OF ASAR, ASET AND HERU: An Ancient Egyptian Legend (For Children)   Now for the first time, the most ancient myth of Ancient Egypt comes alive for children. Inspired by the books *The Asarian Resurrection: The Ancient Egyptian Bible* and *The Mystical Teachings of The Asarian Resurrection, The Story of Asar, Aset and Heru* is an easy to understand and thrilling tale which inspired

MAAT PHILOSOPHY & The Wisdom of Maati

the children of Ancient Egypt to aspire to greatness and righteousness.   If you and your child have enjoyed stories like *The Lion King* and *Star Wars you will love The Story of Asar, Aset and Heru*. Also, if you know the story of Jesus and Krishna you will discover than Ancient Egypt had a similar myth and that this myth carries important spiritual teachings for living a fruitful and fulfilling life. This book may be used along with *The Parents Guide To The Asarian Resurrection Myth: How to Teach Yourself and Your Child the Principles of Universal Mystical Religion.* The guide provides some background to the Asarian Resurrection myth and it also gives insight into the mystical teachings contained in it which you may introduce to your child. It is designed for parents who wish to grow spiritually with their children and it serves as an introduction for those who would like to study the Asarian Resurrection Myth in depth and to practice its teachings. 41 pages   8.5" X 11"   ISBN: 1-884564-31-3 $12.95

25.   THE PARENTS GUIDE TO THE AUSARIAN RESURRECTION MYTH: How to Teach Yourself and Your Child the Principles of Universal Mystical Religion.   This insightful manual brings for the timeless wisdom of the ancient through the Ancient Egyptian myth of Asar, Aset and Heru and the mystical teachings contained in it for parents who want to guide their children to understand and practice the teachings of mystical spirituality. This manual may be used with the children's storybook *The Story of Asar, Aset and Heru* by Dr. Muata Abhaya Ashby. 5.5"x 8.5"   ISBN: 1-884564-30-5 $14.95

26.   HEALING THE CRIMINAL HEART BOOK 1 Introduction to Maat Philosophy, Yoga and Spiritual Redemption Through the Path of Virtue   Who is a criminal? Is there such a thing as a criminal heart? What is the source of evil and sinfulness and is there any way to rise above it? Is there redemption for those who have committed sins, even the worst crimes?   Ancient Egyptian mystical psychology holds important answers to these questions. Over ten thousand years ago mystical psychologists, the Sages of Ancient Egypt, studied and charted the human mind and spirit and laid out a path which will lead to spiritual redemption, prosperity and Enlightenment.   This introductory volume brings forth the teachings of the Asarian Resurrection, the most important myth of Ancient Egypt, with relation to the faults of human existence: anger, hatred, greed, lust, animosity, discontent, ignorance, egoism jealousy, bitterness, and a myriad of psycho-spiritual ailments which keep a human being in a state of negativity and adversity. 5.5"x 8.5"   ISBN: 1-884564-17-8 $15.95

27.   THEATER & DRAMA OF THE ANCIENT EGYPTIAN MYSTERIES: Featuring the Ancient Egyptian stage play-"The Enlightenment of Hathor' Based on an Ancient Egyptian Drama, The original Theater - Mysticism of the Temple of Hetheru $14.95   By Dr. Muata Ashby

28.   GUIDE TO PRINT ON DEMAND: SELF-PUBLISH FOR PROFIT, SPIRITUAL FULFILLMENT AND SERVICE TO HUMANITY Everyone asks us how we produced so many books in such a short time. Here are the secrets to writing and producing books that uplift humanity and how to get them printed for a fraction of the regular cost. Anyone can become an author even if they have limited funds. All that is necessary is the willingness to learn how the printing and book business work and the desire to follow the special instructions given here for preparing your manuscript format. Then you take your work directly to the non-traditional companies who can produce your books for less than the traditional book printer can. ISBN: 1-884564-40-2 $16.95 U. S.

29.   Egyptian Mysteries: Vol. 1, Shetaut Neter ISBN: 1-884564-41-0 $19.99 What are the Mysteries? For thousands of years the spiritual tradition of Ancient Egypt, S*hetaut Neter,* "The Egyptian Mysteries," "The Secret Teachings," have fascinated, tantalized and amazed the world. At one time exalted and recognized as the highest culture of the world, by Africans, Europeans, Asiatics, Hindus, Buddhists and other cultures of the ancient world, in time it was shunned by the emerging orthodox world religions. Its temples desecrated, its philosophy maligned, its tradition spurned, its philosophy dormant in the mystical *Medu Neter,* the mysterious hieroglyphic texts which hold the secret symbolic meaning that has scarcely been discerned up to now. What are the secrets of *Nehast* {spiritual awakening and emancipation, resurrection}. More than just a literal translation, this volume is for awakening to the secret code *Shetitu* of the teaching which was not deciphered by Egyptologists, nor could be understood by ordinary spiritualists. This book is a reinstatement of the original science made available for our times, to the reincarnated followers of Ancient Egyptian culture and the prospect of spiritual freedom to break the bonds of *Khemn,* "ignorance," and slavery to evil forces: *Såaa* .

182

The Path of Action and Enlightenment

30.   EGYPTIAN MYSTERIES VOL 2: Dictionary of Gods and Goddesses ISBN: 1-884564-23-2 $21.95
This book is about the mystery of neteru, the gods and goddesses of Ancient Egypt (Kamit, Kemet). Neteru
means "Gods and Goddesses." But the Neterian teaching of Neteru represents more than the usual limited
modern day concept of "divinities" or "spirits." The Neteru of Kamit are also metaphors, cosmic principles
and vehicles for the enlightening teachings of Shetaut Neter (Ancient Egyptian-African Religion). Actually
they are the elements for one of the most advanced systems of spirituality ever conceived in human history.
Understanding the concept of neteru provides a firm basis for spiritual evolution and the pathway for viable
culture, peace on earth and a healthy human society.   Why is it important to have gods and goddesses in
our lives? In order for spiritual evolution to be possible, once a human being has accepted that there is
existence after death and there is a transcendental being who exists beyond time and space knowledge,
human beings need a connection to that which transcends the ordinary experience of human life in time and
space and a means to understand the transcendental reality beyond the mundane reality.

31.   EGYPTIAN MYSTERIES VOL. 3 The Priests and Priestesses of Ancient Egypt ISBN: 1-884564-53-4
$22.95 This volume details the path of Neterian priesthood, the joys, challenges and rewards of advanced
Neterian life, the teachings that allowed the priests and priestesses to manage the most long lived
civilization in human history and how that path can be adopted today; for those who want to tread the path
of the Clergy of Shetaut Neter.

32.   THE KING OF EGYPT: The Struggle of Good and Evil for Control of the World and The Human Soul
ISBN 1-8840564-44-5 $18.95   Have you seen movies like The Lion King, Hamlet, The Odyssey, or The
Little Buddha? These have been some of the most popular movies in modern times. The Sema Institute of
Yoga is dedicated to researching and presenting the wisdom and culture of ancient Africa. The Script is
designed to be produced as a motion picture but may be addapted for the theater as well. 160 pages bound
or unbound (specify with your order) $19.95   copyright 1998 By Dr. Muata Ashby

33.   FROM EGYPT TO GREECE: The Kamitan Origins of Greek Culture and Religion ISBN: 1-884564-47-X
$22.95 U.S. FROM EGYPT TO GREECE   This insightful manual is a quick reference to Ancient Egyptian
mythology and philosophy and its correlation to what later became known as Greek and Rome mythology
and philosophy. It outlines the basic tenets of the mythologies and shoes the ancient origins of Greek
culture in Ancient Egypt. This volume also acts as a resource for Colleges students who would like to set
up fraternities and sororities based on the original Ancient Egyptian principles of Sheti and Maat
philosophy. ISBN: 1-884564-47-X $22.95 U.S.

34.   THE FORTY TWO PRECEPTS OF MAAT, THE PHILOSOPHY OF RIGHTEOUS ACTION AND THE
ANCIENT EGYPTIAN WISDOM TEXTS ADVANCED STUDIES This manual is designed for use with
the 1998 Maat Philosophy Class conducted by Dr. Muata Ashby. This is a detailed study of Maat
Philosophy. It contains a compilation of the 42 laws or precepts of Maat and the corresponding principles
which they represent along with the teachings of the ancient Egyptian Sages relating to each. Maat
philosophy was the basis of Ancient Egyptian society and government as well as the heart of Ancient
Egyptian myth and spirituality. Maat is at once a goddess, a cosmic force and a living social doctrine,
which promotes social harmony and thereby paves the way for spiritual evolution in all levels of society.
ISBN: 1-884564-48-8 $16.95 U.S.

Music Based on the Prt M Hru and other Kemetic Texts

Available on Compact Disc $14.99 and Audio Cassette $9.99

Adorations to the Goddess

Music for Worship of the Goddess

**NEW Egyptian Yoga Music CD
by Sehu Maa
Ancient Egyptian Music CD**
Instrumental Music played on reproductions of Ancient Egyptian Instruments– Ideal for <u>meditation</u> and reflection on the Divine and for the practice of spiritual programs and <u>Yoga exercise sessions.</u>

©1999 By Muata Ashby
CD $14.99 –

MERIT'S INSPIRATION
**NEW Egyptian Yoga Music CD
by Sehu Maa
Ancient Egyptian Music CD**
Instrumental Music played on

reproductions of Ancient Egyptian Instruments– Ideal for <u>meditation</u> and reflection on the Divine and for the practice of spiritual programs and <u>Yoga exercise sessions.</u>
©1999 By
Muata Ashby
CD $14.99 –
UPC# 761527100429

ANORATIONS TO RA AND HETHERU
**NEW Egyptian Yoga Music CD
By Sehu Maa (Muata Ashby)
Based on the Words of Power of Ra and HetHeru**
played on reproductions of Ancient Egyptian Instruments **Ancient Egyptian Instruments used: Voice, Clapping, Nefer Lute, Tar Drum, Sistrums, Cymbals –** The Chants, Devotions, Rhythms and Festive Songs Of the Neteru – Ideal for meditation, and devotional singing and dancing.
©1999 By Muata Ashby
CD $14.99 –
UPC# 761527100221

SONGS TO ASAR ASET AND HERU
NEW
Egyptian Yoga Music CD
By Sehu Maa

played on reproductions of Ancient Egyptian Instruments— The Chants, Devotions, Rhythms and Festive Songs Of the Neteru - Ideal for meditation, and devotional singing and dancing.
Based on the Words of Power of Asar (Asar), Aset (Aset) and Heru (Heru) Om Asar Aset Heru is the third in a series of musical explorations of the Kemetic (Ancient Egyptian) tradition of music. Its ideas are based on the Ancient Egyptian Religion of Asar, Aset and Heru and it is designed for listening, meditation and worship. ©1999 By Muata Ashby
CD $14.99 –
UPC# 761527100122

HAARI OM: ANCIENT EGYPT MEETS INDIA IN MUSIC
NEW Music CD
By Sehu Maa

The Chants, Devotions, Rhythms and Festive Songs Of the Ancient Egypt and India, harmonized and played on reproductions of ancient instruments along with modern instruments and beats. Ideal for meditation, and devotional singing and dancing.

Haari Om is the fourth in a series of musical explorations of the Kemetic (Ancient Egyptian) and Indian traditions of music, chanting and devotional spiritual practice. Its ideas are based on the Ancient Egyptian Yoga spirituality and Indian Yoga spirituality.
©1999 By Muata Ashby
CD $14.99 –
UPC# 761527100528

RA AKHU: THE GLORIOUS LIGHT
NEW
Egyptian Yoga Music CD
By Sehu Maa
The fifth collection of original music compositions based on the Teachings and Words of The Trinity, the God Asar and the Goddess Nebethet, the Divinity Aten, the God Heru, and the Special Meditation Hekau or Words of Power of Ra from the Ancient Egyptian Tomb of Seti I and more... played on reproductions of Ancient Egyptian Instruments and modern instruments - Ancient Egyptian Instruments used: Voice, Clapping, Nefer Lute, Tar Drum, Sistrums, Cymbals
– The Chants, Devotions, Rhythms and Festive Songs Of the Neteru – Ideal for meditation, and devotional singing and dancing.
©1999 By Muata Ashby
CD $14.99 –
UPC# 761527100825

GLORIES OF THE DIVINE MOTHER
Based on the hieroglyphic text of the
worship of Goddess Net.
The Glories of The Great Mother
©2000 Muata Ashby
CD $14.99 UPC# 761527101129`

The Path of Action and Enlightenment

Order Form

Telephone orders: Call Toll Free: 1(305) 378-6253. Have your AMEX, Optima, Visa or MasterCard ready.

Fax orders: 1-(305) 378-6253   E-MAIL ADDRESS: Semayoga@aol.com

Postal Orders: Sema Institute of Yoga, P.O. Box 570459, Miami, Fl. 33257. USA.

Please send the following books and / or tapes.

ITEM

_____Cost $_____

_____Cost $_____

_____Cost $_____

_____Cost $_____

_____Cost $_____

Total $_____

Name:_____

Physical Address:_____

City:_____ State:_____ Zip:_____

Sales tax: Please add 6.5% for books shipped to Florida addresses

_____Shipping: $6.50 for first book and .50¢ for each additional

_____Shipping: Outside US $5.00 for first book and $3.00 for each additional

_____Payment:_____

_____Check -Include Driver License #:

_____

_____Credit card: _____ Visa, _____ MasterCard, _____ Optima,

_____ AMEX.

Card number:_____

Name on card:_____ Exp. date:_____ /_____

Copyright 1995-2005 Dr. R. Muata Abhaya Ashby

Sema Institute of Yoga

P.O.Box 570459, Miami, Florida, 33257

(305) 378-6253 Fax: (305) 378-6253